The Secret
Language of Trees

The Secret Language of Trees

Gill Davies

Forewords by
Dr Nick Atkinson, Woodland Trust
Tony Kirkham, Royal Botanic Gardens, Kew

First published in 2018
by Worth Press Ltd, Bath, England.
worthpress@btconnect.com

© Worth Press Ltd, 2018

British Library Cataloguing in Publication Data.
A catalogue record for this book is available from the British Library.

ISBN: 978-1-84931-155-7

10 9 8 7 6 5 4 3 2 1

Publisher's Note: While every effort has been made to ensure that the information herein is complete and accurate, the publisher and author make no representations or warranties either expressed or implied of any kind with respect to this book to the reader. Neither the author nor the publisher shall be liable or responsible for any damage, loss or expense of any kind arising out of information contained in this book. The thoughts or opinions expressed in this book represent the personal views of the author and not necessarily those of the publisher. Further, the publisher takes no responsibility for third party Websites or their content.

The images used in this book come from either the public domain or from the public commons unless otherwise stated. Every effort has been made to trace copyright holders and seek permission to use illustrative material. The publishers wish to apologise for any inadvertent errors or omissions and would be glad to rectify these in future editions.

The author, publishers and writers of the forewords accept no responsibility for the contents and information contained in this book, neither can they endorse any of the medical information, some of which is folklore or ancient and incomplete knowledge. It is included as a point of interest, not as a recommendation. Contradictions may apply if suffering certain conditions or already taking prescribed medications, so further research and advice should be sought from a qualified doctor before considering the consumption of any foraged material, be it berries, bark, leaves, flowers, roots or mushrooms.

Editorial Direction: Cristina Galimberti
Design and layout: Arati Devasher, aratidevasher.com
Editing and picture research: Meredith MacArdle

Printed and bound in China

Contents

Notes from a Conservationist

Stepping into a woodland is to enter a secret world linking directly to our past. Ancient woodlands, those which are known to have existed since the earliest maps and most likely for thousands of years, bear the unmistakable signs of generations of human exploitation. Trees provided our main sources of fuel and materials and woodlands have worked hard over many centuries. To chance upon an ancient ash coppice stool is to come face to face with perhaps a thousand years of human industry that has also shaped and supported the wildlife around it.

Trees are foundation species, the scaffold upon which nature's stage is built. Until people began building pyramids and then tower blocks, trees were the tallest freestanding structures on the planet. All terrestrial life has evolved with the tree as its vertical measure, and so much of it centres on trees. For example, well over 2,000 species are known to depend on oak, at least 300 of which do so entirely. Trees are not just individuals, they are complete ecosystems, each an island of biodiversity in its own right.

Outside woodland, trees define landscapes from the Serengeti in Africa to the South Downs in the UK. Many of the most ancient trees are found in this non-woodland setting: the European churchyard yews of pre-Christian antiquity, the great gnarled oaks of the parkland and the farmland ashes that replaced the elms when Dutch elm disease destroyed the vista in the 1970s. Madagascar's strange baobabs sprout from the arid soils like disembodied elephant legs; Spain's *dehesa* groves (a type of agroforestry) of ancient cork oaks and olives mark centuries in pursuit of life's finer pleasures; bristlecone pines in the Western USA's Great Basin eke out the longest known lives in the harshest of conditions.

Our fate is intimately intertwined with that of trees. Now more than ever we put pressure on them, from development, intensive agriculture, pollution and water stress. Less than 40 per cent of the world's forests remain, the rest cleared for logging, unsustainable agriculture and more recently the creation of vast palm oil plantations. Small wonder we are on, perhaps even beyond, the brink of the sixth mass extinction event in the Earth's history and the first to be caused by another species. Climate change will transform the world's forests and the species they shelter but trees and woods can also help us to adapt through the many benefits they provide.

There is a tendency in our increasingly goal-driven world to only afford space and time for those things that provide us with a measurable benefit. This risks reducing trees to their functions in absorbing carbon dioxide, stabilizing soils and providing urban shade, a dangerous path that leads inevitably to the conclusion that the 'tree that pays is the tree that stays'. It is the reason why, when farmers no longer depended on pollarded hedgerow trees for timber, fuel and fodder and when efficiency demanded ever larger fields, hundreds of thousands of kilometres of hedgerows and the centuries-old 'standards' they contained were grubbed up during the twentieth century. It is also why during that same period half of our remaining ancient woodland was also felled and replanted with exotic conifer species, whose economic value was deemed the greater.

The threats to our trees and woods are palpable. New pests and diseases arrive annually, some with the potential to rival the great elm epidemic. Ash dieback, caused by a fungus native to Southeast Asia, is decimating ash populations in Europe. In North America all six native ash species are now classified as endangered by the International Union for the Conservation of Nature, five of them critically. Billions of trees there have been killed by the emerald ash borer, an exquisite bark beetle that in its native Asian range is little more than a minor irritation to its co-adapted hosts.

All of this, and more, is why the conservation of trees and woods is so important. This book provides further glimpses of the wonderful things they are. Play the tree ID game next time you are out, whether it's a country walk with family or the commute to work. See how the form of a tree tells you about its past: is it spreading (open grown) or searching for the light (woodland)? Does it show signs of past management through coppicing (multiple stems at ground level) or pollarding (cut higher up to keep new growth away from livestock)? Above all, cherish the tree-scape: it is the foundation on which we all depend.

—Nick Atkinson, Woodland Trust, Grantham, March 2018

Notes from a Botanist

I can still clearly remember my first meeting with a horse chestnut one Friday afternoon in early spring when I was at primary school. My schoolteacher brought into the classroom from the playground an enormous bunch of horse chestnut twigs bearing the large, swollen, sticky buds. She placed them in a vase filled with water and told us all that this tree at the end of the playground was about to signal the start of spring and with the warmth of the classroom the twigs would all be in full leaf by Monday morning. I did not believe her and on the following Monday morning I rushed into school earlier than usual, ran up the broad staircase and into the classroom to prove her wrong. I was mesmerized by what I saw: a floral display of twigs covered with vibrant, lush, green leaves. I was so surprised that a bunch of twigs could do this so quickly. My teacher then told me why it was called the horse chestnut: because of the horseshoe-shaped leaf scars on the young twigs. From that day on I wanted to learn more about trees and had my career path set for a world of dendrology.

Many years later I learned that this was not where the common name came from, but that the tree's conkers were crushed, mixed with water, and fed to horses in Macedonia where the tree is native, to cure their colic. The latter story may not be true as well, and I realized that it does not really matter which fact is true or false, so long as it captures the imagination as it did mine. Since then I have become the curator of the Arboretum tree collection at the Royal Botanic Gardens, Kew, a top job for a tree person. The Arboretum is one big storybook where every tree is a page and has an interesting story to tell.

Trees are amazing works of nature that influence our everyday lives in every aspect, sometimes without us realizing. Not only do they look beautiful and provide us with a multitude of seasonal attributes to brighten up our lives, but they also create a living, changing, backdrop that softens and greens our landscapes in towns and cities, making, cleaning and cooling the air that we breathe. For example, a young oak tree, about 100 years old, will, on a sunny day, absorb and convert around 9 kilograms of carbon dioxide into 7 kilograms of oxygen, enough for about five people to breathe for that one day. The tree will also filter out bacteria, fungal spores, dust and other harmful substances – providing a cleaner environment for all of us to live in. At the same time, it will take up about 200 to 400 litres of water through its roots, reducing storm water runoff, preventing flooding and the erosion of unstable soils.

Research has shown that more trees and woodlands make people happier and less stressed, with hospital recovery times reduced, property prices increased, crime reduced and our life expectancy going up, all because of the tree-scape.

This oak tree, which provides all of these benefits, also enhances biodiversity by providing a habitat and food for over 200 different species of insects, which in turn provide food for a variety of birds. These birds will roost and nest in the cavities and crevices of the tree as will many mammals like bats and squirrels. Oaks also play host to a number of wood-rotting fungi and friendly mycorrhizal fungi that break down the fallen leaves of deciduous trees, providing another type of habitat for invertebrates and mammals.

Trees offer many cultural links to the wider environment and historically have been a source of timber for house- and shipbuilding, fuel for heating and cooking, fruit for eating, leaves for medicinal properties as well as having many other uses.

Trees capture the imagination of everyone. We need to continue to learn more about how they have shaped the world and the benefits they provide us with today in our daily lives, and hopefully we will give them the respect that they deserve.

—Tony Kirkham, Kew, March 2018

Fir

HE *ABIES* family includes more than 50 evergreen coniferous species – many veritable giants – such as Frazer, Frazier or Fraser's fir, balsam fir, eastern fir, southern fir, white fir, noble fir, California red and Pacific silver fir. All have needle-like leaves and erect, cylindrical cones raised up like candles. Fir trees can live for several hundred years. Similar to pines and spruces, firs can be distinguished by their needles, which (like spruces) attach individually to branches but are flat and soft. The North American Douglas fir, often used for timber, is not a true fir tree.

LATIN NAME *Abies*

HABITAT
Firs are found in mountainous regions through much of central and North America, Europe, North Africa and Asia.
They are well adapted to snowy regions because their short, stiff branches and pointed tops can shed snow without breaking.
Siberian firs are able to withstand temperatures as low as -45°C (-50°F).

MEANINGS
Fir: time.
Evergreen: can mean poverty.
Evergreen trees, garlands and wreaths have symbolized eternal life since the days of the ancient Egyptians and Chinese.

To the Druids, firs represented truth because they are so strong and straight.

SECRETS AND SPECIAL ASSOCIATIONS
Many Native American peoples link fir trees to spirituality.
Scandinavian legends tell of a boy, lost on Christmas Eve, who was found sheltering under a fir. Ice on the tree shone in the sunlight, so the villagers took firs home to recreate the spectacle, creating the Christmas tree tradition.
Fir Christmas trees became popular in Germany, and were brought by Prince Albert to 19th-century England. They then became a worldwide Yuletide feature.

INTRIGUING INFORMATION
Every year fir trees produce one whorl of branches so if a tree is 60 years old it will have 60 branch whorls.
The silver fir's soft wood is easily worked and is popular for carpentry; its bark yields a high-quality turpentine, Burgundy pitch and other resin products.

O Christmas tree, O Christmas tree,
How lovely are thy branches!
Not only green when summer's here
But in the coldest time of year.
O Christmas tree, O Christmas tree,
How lovely are thy branches!
Translation from the German carol, 'O Tannenbaum'

*Pristine white acacia petals shed an enshrouding pale-green
aura. Mild evening breezes made ... the acacia petals dance
and whirl, filling the woods with a soft rustle.*
Mo Yan (1955–), China

Have the people make an Ark of acacia wood.
The Bible, Exodus 25:10

Acacia or Wattle

HE FLOWERS brandish dense, globular heads, countless stamens set amid soft clusters of fuzzy gold or elongated spikes. Ants often nest inside their hollow thorns, revelling in the tree sap, a good source of sugar and water; sometimes the ants 'milk' sap-sucking insects like aphids or scale insects. *Acacia drepanolobium* is called the whistling thorn because if ants make holes in its bulbous thorns, it makes a whistling sound in the wind. The kangaroo thorn (*Acacia paradoxa*), grown for Easter displays in Australia, also serves as a hedge plant or sand dune stabilizer. Spiky, sweet thorn *Acacia karroo* flourishes in Africa's grasslands where giraffes can manipulate their tongues around the spines to munch the fresh, tasty leaves. Pollinators include beetles, flies, moths, and butterflies.

LATIN NAME *Acacia*

HABITAT

Acacias grow in a wide range of habitats: alpine settings, rainforests, woodlands, grasslands, forests, coastal dunes and deserts.

It is Australia's largest genus of flowering plants, with almost 1,000 species found there and on Pacific islands.

More than 500 species flourish in tropical and subtropical regions of America, Asia, and Africa, plus warmer temperate zones in Europe. Of the 70 American species, nearly half are native to Mexico.

HISTORY

Australian acacias may have evolved their fire resistance about 20 million years ago.

MEANINGS

Chaste love.

SECRETS AND SPECIAL ASSOCIATIONS

If any animals manage to brave the thorns and chew on acacia leaves, the trees create poisonous chemicals to deter the browsers. The leaves fill with poison and release ethylene gas, which warns nearby trees and stimulates them to take the same precautions.

INTRIGUING INFORMATION

A sweet gum that oozes from the trunk is enjoyed by humans and lesser bushbabies.

The thorns have been used as sewing needles.

Some acacia seeds can be ground into flour.

The timber has been used for making fences (keeping lions from Masaii villages in Kenya), rafts, tools, furniture, oars, gunstocks and musical instruments.

Its tannin is used for glues and leather.

Gum Arabic (made from some species) is a thickener for food, medicine, cosmetics and more.

Early European settlers in Australia made wattle and daub huts from acacia.

Maple

OST MAPLES trees grow to about 10–45 metres (33–148 feet). Mainly deciduous trees, they blossom with green, yellow, orange or red flowers in late winter or early spring – around the time the leaves reappear – and several species make a joyous flourish with nectar and pollen much appreciated by bees. With a range of colourful leaves, in general all maples are renowned for their glorious autumn show. Norway maple, silver maple, Japanese maple and red maple are especially popular.

LATIN NAME *Acer*

HABITAT
Most of the 128 species are native to Asia, with a few in Europe, northern Africa, and North America. Only *Acer laurinum* reaches the Southern Hemisphere.

HISTORY
Maple syrup was first collected and used by indigenous North Americans, and then adopted by European settlers, who gradually refined production methods.

MEANINGS
In the language of flowers maple means 'reserve'.
The maple symbolizes strength and endurance.

SECRETS AND SPECIAL ASSOCIATIONS
It is the national tree of Canada; a maple leaf is on the Canadian flag and coat of arms.
Hidden within the timber, visible when sawn, are highly decorative grain patterns, called flame, burl, quilt and birdseye.
The wood is an excellent carrier of sound waves and serves in musical instruments as varied as cellos, guitars, bassoons, drums and drumsticks.
When under attack, maple trees possibly send airborne signals to warn other trees of impending danger so that they can increase their chemical weapon production or activate other defence mechanisms.

INTRIGUING INFORMATION
The winged fruits (called keys, helicopters, whirlybirds or polynoses) are shaped to spin as they fall and carry the seeds a considerable distance on the wind.
During World War II the US Army developed an airdrop carrier based on the maple seed.
Maples make excellent bonsai subjects.
Viewing the brilliant colours of maples in the autumn is a much-appreciated custom in Japan, Korea and Canada.
Maple is an important source of syrup, wood, paper and charcoal.
Hard maple makes bowling pins, bowling alley lanes, pool cues and baseball bats.

Autumn is a second spring when every leaf is a flower.
Albert Camus (1913–60), France/Algeria

… colored and glowing like oak and maple in autumn,
when the sun gold is richest.
John Muir (1838–1914) Scotland/USA

It is not so much for its beauty that the forest makes a claim upon men's hearts, as for that subtle something, that quality of air, that emanation from old trees, that so wonderfully changes and renews a weary spirit.
Robert Louis Stevenson (1850–94), Scotland

The tree is a slow, enduring force straining to win the sky.
Antoine de Saint-Exupéry (1900–44), France

Sycamore

LSO KNOWN as the sycamore maple, this robust tree is among the planet's oldest and may have existed for over 100 million years. A species of maple, it can grow to 35 metres (115 feet) and live for some 500 years. Ancient trunks may split or assume twisted, contorted forms while smooth, marbled bark becomes cracked and plated. Small, green-yellow flowers hang in spikes; in autumn five-lobed leaves turn deep gold as winged seeds spin down like little helicopters. Squirrels, wood ducks (and raccoons in the USA) inhabit its branches where aphids attract ladybirds, hoverflies and birds. The leaves are eaten by caterpillars of the sycamore moth plus plumed and maple prominent moths while, in some countries, hummingbirds relish its nectar. The seeds are eaten by birds and voles. Sycamore wood is one of many that are nicknamed lacewood. The sycamore mentioned in the Bible and in ancient Egypt is actually a different tree, the sycamore fig.

LATIN NAME *Acer pseudoplatanus*

HABITAT

Native to central, eastern and southern Europe. Introduced into Britain, Australasia, the Americas, Madeira and Azores.

Thrives near rivers, streams, lakes, railway lines and roadside verges.

This is the most common maple in Europe.

HISTORY

The Classical Greek physician, Hippocrates, taught his medical students under a sycamore tree on the island of Kos.

In Pennsylvania, USA, a 168-year-old sycamore is said to have sheltered George Washington's soldiers during the 1777 Battle of Brandywine.

England's Tolpuddle Martyrs' Tree – a sycamore – dates from 1680. Here six agricultural labourers formed a union in 1834, and were transported to Australia.

MEANINGS

In the language of flowers: curiosity.

Also symbolizes divinity, eternity and strength.

SECRETS AND SPECIAL ASSOCIATIONS

Sycamore is associated with a wide range of fungi; some may live within its root cells.

INTRIGUING INFORMATION

Flooring, veneer, furniture, barrels, violin parts, whistles and carved Welsh love spoons are all made from sycamore.

It is an energy crop for biofuel systems.

A sycamore tree produces over 10,000 wind-dispersed seeds every year.

Its sap can be used to make beer.

Easy to saw or split with an axe, it provides a good, hot fuel.

The nectar makes excellent honey.

Baobab

ERHAPS THE world's largest succulent, the majestic baobab (or upside-down tree) towers over scrublands and is an African icon. Huge, bulbous stems store massive amounts of water, helping it cope with drought. Tangled branches ooze with large (usually white), short-lived, smelly flowers; these are pollinated at night by fruit bats. The fruits form big pods, rich in vitamin C, called 'monkey bread'. Some baobabs have vast, hollow trunks that have housed post offices, jails, bus stops and even pubs! Its nooks and crannies hide reptiles, insects and bats; baboons, antelopes, monkeys, elephants and warthogs relish the seedpods; weaverbirds build nests in the canopy while African honeybees, mottled spinetails, ground hornbills and barn owls tuck into its hollows. The Australian tree called baobab is a different species.

LATIN NAME *Adansonia digitata*

HABITAT
Dry zones of Madagascar, 32 African nations, Arabia.
It was introduced in ancient times to south Asia and during the colonial era to the Caribbean.

HISTORY
This species is 200 million years old.
Its Latin name honours the 18th-century French naturalist Michel Adanson.

MEANINGS
The tree of life; symbol of strength, power and grace.

SECRETS AND SPECIAL ASSOCIATIONS
The tree is revered in Senegal, where it is the national symbol. In some African cultures, deceased relatives are buried at the base of baobabs, and it is believed that the trees become imbued with their souls.
One legend tells how, when the baobab was planted by God, it kept walking, so God pulled it up and replanted it upside down to stop it moving.

INTRIGUING INFORMATION
In South Africa, the Glencoe Baobab had a circumference of about 47 metres (154 ft) but then split into two separate trunks.
Until it fell in 2017, the Sunland Big Baobab had a bar within its hollow trunk in which 16 drinkers could fit.
Baobabs can live for up to 5,000 years.
It is nicknamed 'dead rat tree' after its furry fruits that seem to hang by their tails. Inside is a hard, coconut-like shell containing the fruit pulp.
The fibrous bark provides fuel, rope, bracelets, glue, baskets, mats, fishing nets, sacks, dyes and clothing.
Baobab is the only fruit in the world that dries naturally on the branch.

Wisdom is like a baobab tree; no one individual can embrace it.
African proverb

I pointed out to the little prince that baobabs were not little bushes,
but, on the contrary, trees as big as castles.
Antoine de Saint-Exupéry (1900–44), France

In life you have to do three things: make a son, write a book, plant a tree.
Various attributions include Zen Buddhist sources,
the Babylonian Talmud, Pablo Picasso, Spain, José Maria de Eça de Queirós,
Portugal, and Compay Segundo quoting José Martí, Cuba.

This is the weather the cuckoo likes,
And so do I;
When showers betumble the chestnut spikes,
And nestlings fly;
Thomas Hardy (1840–1928), England

Horse Chestnut and Buckeye

HORSE CHESTNUTS shoot up quickly and may reach 30 metres (98 feet) high. They can live for 300 years. The greyish-green or brown bark has corky, wart-like eruptions and thick, knobby spines. In late spring, creamy-yellow or white flowers with scarlet-tinged centres or yellow mottling form showy, upright clusters. Horse chestnut fruits are not the edible chestnut we enjoy roasting (see pages 32–33 for these) but do provide prize-winning conkers, eagerly gathered in autumn for playground competitions. When the leaves fall, the stalk breaks away, leaving a horseshoe-shaped scar with 'nail holes' so this may be the origin of its name. North American horse chestnuts are called buckeyes because their large seeds resemble deer eyes.

LATIN NAME *Aesculus*
Aesculus hippocastanum (horse chestnut)
*Aesculus glabra (*Ohio buckeye)

HABITAT
Temperate Asia, Europe and North America. Seven species are native to North America; six are Eurasian.

HISTORY
The European or common horse chestnut is believed to have spread from the Balkan regions of Eastern Europe.

During World War I British children were asked to collect conkers as a source of starch, but they were actually used to make acetone, which is needed in the manufacture of cordite for the munitions industry.

In the 1840 US election, candidate William Henry Harrison from Ohio portrayed himself as a 'man of the people' sitting in a buckeye log cabin; Ohio became known as the Buckeye State.

MEANINGS
Luxury.

SECRETS AND SPECIAL ASSOCIATIONS
It was said to be lucky to have a rabbit foot and a horse chestnut in your right pocket.

The buds of red horse chestnut trees are said to soothe those who constantly worry about their loved ones, while those from the white chestnut stop unwanted, repetitive thoughts.

INTRIGUING INFORMATION
The wood is used for crates and packing cases.

Children often string together the chocolate-brown seeds into necklaces.

Leached of their toxin, the seeds were eaten by Japan's Jōmon people for 4,000 years.

Native Americans crushed the seeds and threw the mash into still water to stun or kill fish.

Albeit mildly poisonous to many animals, deer and wild boar safely consume them and ground-up horse chestnuts have been fed to horses (and cattle) as a stimulant, to make their coats shine and as a cough remedy.

Alder

GENERALLY GROWING near streams, rivers, watercourses and wetlands, most alders are deciduous with wind-pollinated catkins that provide an early source of nectar and pollen for bees, as well as food for butterflies and moths (like small pearl-bordered fritillaries and chequered skippers). Some species support caterpillars such as alder kittens, pebble hook-tips, autumnal and blue-bordered carpet moths. This is the only deciduous tree to develop woody cones, which, when ripe, contain countless small seeds, often eaten by birds such as siskins, redpolls and goldfinches. Alder roots enrich the soil by fixing nitrogen from the air, while damp alder woodlands encourage mosses, lichens and fungi – and alder roots make perfect nest sites for otters. The tree has many associations with magic and fairies.

LATIN NAME *Almus*

HABITAT

North temperate zones of Europe – across Russia to Siberia, plus the Caucasus, Iran, Turkey and North Africa. A few species grow in Central America and in the Andes.

Grows most happily beside water.

HISTORY

Alder was sacred to the Druids.

In Norse legend the first man and woman were made from ash and alder.

Druids associated this tree with the fox; the Norse associated it with the raven.

MEANINGS

Giving and nurturing; care and generosity.

SECRETS AND SPECIAL ASSOCIATIONS

Because it makes good dyes, alder is associated with goddesses of spinning.

Celtic countries associated it with death and used alder rods to measure corpses and graves.

Alders are said to encourage people to face up to things they have hitherto been avoiding.

When cut, the wood appears to bleed and many people feared the trees.

The green shoots make fine whistles, once said to be able to 'whistle up the wind'.

INTRIGUING INFORMATION

When immersed in water, alder wood becomes hard as stone, resisting decay, and so is good for boats, sluice gates, troughs and pipes.

Some of the piles supporting Venice were made from alder trees 1200 years ago.

It was once used to make clogs.

Alder bark and wood are used to tan leather.

The green dye from the flowers was used to dye clothes and camouflage outlaws such as Robin Hood.

A red dye can also be made from the outer bark and a yellow dye from the inner bark.

*A tree trunk the size of a man grows from a
blade as thin as a hair.*
Laozi (604–531 BCE), China

*Learn character from trees, values from roots
and change from leaves.*
Tasneem Hameed, Pakistan

*We have nothing to fear and a great deal to learn from
trees, that vigorous and pacific tribe which without
stint produces strengthening essences for us, soothing
balms, and in whose gracious company we spend so
many cool, silent, and intimate hours.*

Marcel Proust (1871–1922), France

Monkey Puzzle Tree

ALSO KNOWN as the monkey tail tree, Chilean pine, and pehuén, this angular evergreen has stiff, symmetrical branches covered by rigid, overlapping, scale-like leaves that may survive for more than two decades. Its unusual crown grows from the trunk in whorls, with young specimens sporting a pyramidal, Christmas-tree-shaped pinnacle that, in the mature tree, assumes a distinctive umbrella canopy. It can live for 1,000 years and reach some 30 to 40 metres (100 to 130 feet) high. Because of its longevity, the monkey puzzle tree is regarded as a living fossil.

LATIN NAME *Araucaria araucana*
The name is derived from the native Araucanian people who used the seeds in Chile.

HABITAT
Native to Chile, Argentina and lower slopes of south-central Andes, enjoying well-drained, acidic, volcanic soil. Today grows in Western Europe, North American coastal areas, New Zealand and southeastern Australia.
Enjoys well-drained, slightly acidic soil.

HISTORY
Fossils in the Petrified Forest National Park of Arizona, USA show that these trees were once abundant in the Northern Hemisphere.
The tree flourished 150 to 200 million years ago and dinosaurs would have roamed among monkey puzzle forests.

MEANINGS
It does not have an 'official' meaning but is associated with conundrums and challenges.

SECRETS AND SPECIAL ASSOCIATIONS
This is the national tree of Chile.
It is sacred to some Mapuche Native American tribes and to the Chilean Pehuenche people.

It grows on the slopes of volcanoes and, with fire-resistant bark, can survive lava flows.
It is considered unlucky to talk if under a monkey puzzle – you might even grow a monkey's tail.
Planting a monkey puzzle by a graveyard prevents the devil from joining a burial.

INTRIGUING INFORMATION
Its seeds are dispersed by jays, slender-billed parakeets, squirrels and the long-haired grass mouse who buries the seeds whole, helping them germinate.
The tree is home to more than seventy types of insects that live nowhere else.
It is now an endangered species with felling strictly prohibited.
The almond-sized seeds are still harvested and can be enjoyed raw, boiled or roasted.
In South America the Mapuche people distill an alcoholic cider called chavid from the seeds.
It gained its common name when a 19th-century British commentator said, 'It would puzzle a monkey to climb that!'

Madrone

ARBUTUS MENZIESII, also called tick tree and bearberry, is a truly ornamental hardwood. It has red, flaking bark and a froth of gorgeous white spring flowers which scent the air like lilac ... followed by edible, red, strawberry-like berries which in time develop hooked barbs that latch onto animals for greater dispersal. Deer adore madrone berries, as do (depending on location) robins, pigeons, thrushes, cedar waxwings, quail, raccoons, ring-tailed cats and bears. Mature trunks attract woodpeckers while bees and butterflies flock to its blossom. Madrones have been described as mystical, inspiring, sensual and magnificent. These trees twist to follow the sun, creating fantastic forms. In summer the old bark peels away to reveal a glistening new surface – pale green or yellow and silky smooth, or satin-sheened and silver-striped. In time, this new layer turns orange-red or deep crimson and then will, in turn, peel away so there is a constant cycle of texture and colour.

LATIN NAME *Arbutus menziesii*
(Pacific madrone)
A. unedo (Strawberry tree)
A. andrachne (Greek strawberry tree)

HABITAT
Warm temperate regions.
A. menziesii and other American species: North America especially the Pacific Northwest.
A. unedo: Mediterranean, western Europe, Ireland.
They may thrive on rocky, arid slopes.

HISTORY
Arbutus menziesii is named after Scottish botanist Archibald Menzies.
The Roman naturalist Pliny the Elder thought that the strawberry tree, known as unedo even then, was so named because people could only manage to eat one of the unpleasant fruits (*unum edo*).

MEANINGS
Esteem, but not love. Integrity, wisdom.

SECRETS AND SPECIAL ASSOCIATIONS
An *Arbutus unedo* comprises part of Spanish Madrid's coat of arms; a statue of a bear eating the fruit of the tree stands in the city centre and its image appears on crests.
In Canadian Saanich legends, the madrone saved people after a Great Flood by providing an anchor on a mountain.
Native Americans regard it as sacred.

INTRIGUING INFORMATION
Madrone is so dense that freshly cut wood sinks in water. It burns hot and long, surpassing even oak.
The fruit is used for cider, brandy and madroño liqueur, and fishing bait.

If a tree dies, plant another in its place.
Carl Linnaeus (1707–78), Sweden

But though ruddy the berry and snowy the flower
That brighten together the arbutus bower …
Alfred Perceval Graves (1846–1931), Ireland/England

*Trees are the pillars of the world; when the last trees are
cut, the sky will fall above us.*
Native American saying

Birch

ITH THEIR decorative, patterned bark, some with paper-like, thin plates, birches are stunning in winter with various hues earning the trees their common names of white, black, grey, silver and yellow birch. Longer silver birch shoots bear male catkins. Shorter ones produce female catkins that eventually disintegrate to release the seeds. Birds in birch woodland include robins, willow warblers, chaffinches, tree pipits, nightingales, woodcock, redpolls and green woodpeckers. At the same time, some 105 butterflies and moth larvae munch away on birch foliage – many feeding almost exclusively on this. In total, nearly 500 insect species may be found on silver and downy birch including 106 beetles. Down below in the dappled shade, thrive mosses, grasses, primroses, violets, bluebells and anemones.

LATIN NAME *Betula*
Betula pendula (silver birch)
Betula pubescens (downy or white birch)

HABITAT

Silver birch hails from Europe and Southwest Asia but has reached Siberia, China, Turkey, north Iran and more temperate regions of Australia. Its North America introduction is called the European white birch. It is one of the first trees to colonize bare land or appear after a forest fire.

Downy birch (abundant in northern Europe and Asia) is one of very few trees native to Greenland and the only tree to form woodlands in Iceland.

Silver birches prefer drier, sandy soils; downy birches enjoy wet, poorly drained clay and peat bogs.

MEANINGS

In the language of flowers, birch means meekness.
To the Celts it symbolized growth, renewal, stability, initiation and adaptability.

SECRETS AND SPECIAL ASSOCIATIONS

In Ireland birches are associated with the Land of the Dead and Gaelic earthen mounds.

The birch is the national tree of Finland, Sweden and Russia.

During the reconstruction of the Swedish city of Ulmeå after an 1888 conflagration, wide main avenues were built to prevent the spread of future fires and these were lined with birches; it has since been nicknamed the 'city of birches'.

INTRIGUING INFORMATION

Birch's rippled figuring (markings on the cut wood) and streaked timber make attractive veneers and furniture.

Birch is used for racecourse jumps.

Bundles of twigs were used in corporal punishment, hence the term birching.

Native Americans used its flexible, lightweight bark to make canoes, bowls and wigwams.

Birch has a natural resonance and has also been used for making drums, guitar bodies and keyboard mallets.

Birch burns well, even when frozen.

Hornbeam

THE EUROPEAN hornbeam was once called yoke elm since its wood was used for the yokes that enabled oxen to pull a cart. American hornbeam is also known as blue beech or water beech. Hornbeam hedges retain their corrugated leaves all year, providing shelter for woodland creatures. The pale-grey bark has vertical markings. Female catkins develop into papery, winged fruits, called samaras. Many moth caterpillars (including the nut tree tussock, eastern tiger swallowtail, striped hairstreak, red-spotted purple, tiger swallow-tail and case-bearer) grow plump on the leaves while tits, finches, foxes and squirrels relish the autumn seeds. Seeds, buds, and catkins are consumed by ruffed grouse, ring-necked pheasants, ducks and warblers, northern bobwhite and turkeys. In America cottontails, beaver and white-tailed deer relish leaves, twigs and stems.

LATIN NAME *Carpinus betulus* (European or common hornbeam)
Carpinus caroliniana (American hornbeam)

HABITAT
Some 30-40 species in eastern Asia.
Two species are native to Europe.
American hornbeam – eastern North America, including Canada and northern Florida.
All enjoy a warm climate, occurring no higher than 600 metres (1,969 feet), often flourishing in shady mixed oak and beech woodlands or scree forests.

HISTORY
Hornbeams may have been one of the last trees to spread throughout Europe.

MEANINGS
Meekness.

SECRETS AND SPECIAL ASSOCIATIONS
Its tannins may protect the hornbeam's bark from predators.
Hornbeam species provide secret hideaways, roosts and nest sites for birds and small mammals.
Hornbeam is often used by beavers to make their lodges.

INTRIGUING INFORMATION
It cannot compete with some tropical timbers but is one of the hardest temperate woods.
It may be dubbed musclewood or ironwood because it is so sturdy.
Pale, creamy-white hornbeam timber has a flecked grain. Since it is so heavy and strong, it is good for furniture, flooring, butchers' blocks, poles, shoemakers' lasts, cogs for water and windmills, cartwheels, mallets and piano parts.
It is a valued timber for skittle alleys and pins.
Hornbeam burns well – hot and slowly – making excellent firewood and charcoal.
Mature trees may reach 30 metres (98 feet) and can survive over 300 years, their twisted trunks becoming ever more crooked and ridged.

The wood in time waxeth so hard that the toughness and hardness
of it may rather be compared to a horn than unto wood and
therefore it is called hornbeam or hardbeam.
John Gerard (1500s), England

Forests were the first temples of the Divinity, and it is in the forests
that men have grasped the first idea of architecture.
François-Réne de Chateaubriand (1768–1848), France

You are like a chestnut burr, prickly outside, but silky-soft within,
and a sweet kernel, if one can only get at it. Love will make you
show your heart some day, and then the rough burr will fall off.
Louisa May Alcott (1832–88), USA

'The Standing People'.
Native American description of trees

American Chestnut

THIS UPRIGHT tree with a broad, dense crown grows vigorously to reach some 30 metres (98 feet) and has survived for 40 million years … but in the early 1900s an exotic fungus plague attacked 3 to 4 billion trees, almost obliterating the species within 40 years. On healthy specimens, female flowers arrive near catkin bases from late spring. The fragrant, pale green or cream male flowers bloom in July – sprinkled along drooping, noodle-shaped catkins. Prolific nut-bearers, their shiny, brown chestnuts are let loose around the time of the first frost. This has ever been a vital tree for wildlife, feeding some 125 species of butterfly and moth larvae, plus white-tailed deer, blue jays, grouse, turkeys, voles, mice, chipmunks, raccoons, squirrels and wild turkeys. Black bears eat the nuts to fatten up for the winter.

LATIN NAME *Castanea dentata*

HABITAT
Eastern North America

Ranges from southern Ontario and Maine to the Mississippi and from the Atlantic coast to the Appalachian Mountains and Ohio Valley.

HISTORY
Cultivated from 1800, this tree was 'the queen of eastern American forests'.

American chestnut was once one of the most common trees in northeast USA.

It was a popular choice for European pioneers' log cabins.

Blight-resistant hybrids of American and Chinese or Japanese chestnut species are being developed.

Chestnut wood is sometimes reclaimed from old barns.

MEANINGS
Luxury.

SECRETS AND SPECIAL ASSOCIATIONS
This tree returns generous nutrients to the soil.

The fruit or chestnuts are hidden within spiny burrs, secure in a tan 'velvet' casing.

The tree's ability to regenerate from its root collar has helped its survival.

The flowers' sweet fragrance attracts passing insects and pollinators.

INTRIGUING INFORMATION
Its good, strong, straight-grained wood – easy to saw and split – is used for fence posts, furniture, poles, piers, flooring, railroad sleepers (ties), shingles, paper pulp, plywood, musical instruments, caskets and crates.

The high-starch nuts can be milled into flour.

Tannins are extracted from the bark for tanning leather.

The nuts are used in poultry stuffing.

At Thanksgiving and Christmas, roasted chestnuts are sold in city streets.

Cedar of Lebanon

HIS MAJESTIC, evergreen conifer can stretch skyward to 40 metres (130 feet). It has blackish-brown, cracked bark with neat ridges and slightly hairy twigs. The young crown is conical, becoming broader as the years pass by. Needle-like leaves spiral around side shoots in rosettes and clusters. The tree produces cones after some forty years but growth becomes extremely slow after seventy. It flowers in autumn; male cones appear in early September and their female counterparts by the end of that month. Cedar was used for the ships and temples of the ancient Egyptians while its resin served in mummification. There are several other cedars including *C. deodara* which is sacred to Hindus.

LATIN NAME *Cedrus libani*

HABITAT
Native to eastern Mediterranean (Lebanon, Syria and Turkey) and Asia Minor.
Relishes sunny, well-drained, rocky slopes, at altitudes of 1,300 to 3,000 metres (4,300 to 9,800 feet).
It forms forests, and may be blanketed by heavy snow cover at higher altitudes.

HISTORY
The Bible tells how Moses ordered Hebrew priests to use bark of the cedar of Lebanon as a leprosy treatment.
Solomon ordered the timber for the Temple in Jerusalem.

MEANINGS
Incorruptible.
Leaf: symbolizes immortality, tolerance, purification, protection and eternal life.

The prophet Isaiah thought the Lebanon cedar represented pride.

SECRETS AND SPECIAL ASSOCIATIONS
A national emblem of Lebanon, it features on its coat of arms and flag.
Lebanon is sometimes called the Land of the Cedars.
The Epic of Gilgamesh (an ancient Mesopotamian poem) described a sacred cedar forest as the realm of gods; Gilgamesh invaded this, seeking immortality.

INTRIGUING INFORMATION
The hard, durable wood retains a sweet fragrance.
Cedar of Lebanon resin (cedria) and its essential oil (cedrum) are much prized extracts.
It is used as an insect repellent in Lebanon.
An oil (not unlike turpentine) can be obtained.
The fine-grained wood is amazingly durable and immune to insect ravages.
Lebanon cedars are a popular feature in parks surrounding stately homes and mansions.

King Solomon made himself a chariot of the wood of Lebanon ...
The Bible, Song of Solomon 3:9

I tried to discover, in the rumour of forests and waves, words that
other men could not hear, and I pricked up my ears to listen to the
revelation of their harmony.
Gustave Flaubert (1821–80), France

*Love is like a tree: it grows by itself, roots itself
deeply in our being and continues to flourish
over a heart in ruin.*

Victor Hugo (1802–85), France

Cotton Tree or Kapok

ALSO KNOWN as Java cotton, Java kapok, silk-cotton and samauma, this majestic tree is among the largest in the world and may grow 4 metres (13 feet) per year to tower perhaps 61 metres (200 feet) over tropical rainforests. Its mighty trunk buttress flares out across the ground and twists away below the soil for another 30 meters (100 feet), helping the tree to resist all but the most forceful hurricanes and storing reserve water. Major branches, often prickled with large thorns, are up to 1.8 meters (6 feet) thick and support an umbrella crown of foliage. Waxy clusters of pale lemon or ivory flowers proffer golden stamens; smelling like milk, they are a vital nectar and pollen source for honey bees and attract bats by night. Green, boat-shaped seed pods turn a velvety, golden brown and then split to release hundreds of seeds attached to long, silky hairs – the cotton for which this tree is cultivated – light, buoyant and water-resistant but very flammable.

LATIN NAME *Ceiba pentandra*

HABITAT
Mainly native to Mexico, Central America, Caribbean, northern South America.
A few varieties grow in tropical west Africa, southern Asia and the East Indies.

HISTORY
Kapok's buoyant seeds may have been blown across the ocean from the Amazon to Africa.
Mayans thought this was the tree of life whose roots extended to the underworld and whose branches (up which the souls of the dead climbed) held up the heavens.

MEANINGS
Hope, help and strength.
Its Mayan name means 'raised up sky'.
In Trinidad and Tobago folklore, the demon of death is imprisoned in a vast kapok tree.

Its magnificent canopy symbolizes the heavens and its flowers symbolize the stars.

SECRETS AND SPECIAL ASSOCIATIONS
Kapok is the national emblem of Guatemala, Puerto Rico and Equatorial Guinea.
It is the historic symbol of Freetown, Sierra Leone.

INTRIGUING INFORMATION
Its fluffy seed fibre is used by Amazonian tribes to wrap around their blowgun darts, helping force the dart through the tube.
Kapok 'cotton' may serve as filling for pillows, cushions, mattresses, upholstery, insulation and soft toys like teddy bears.
Before the advent of synthetic materials it was used in life jackets.
The seed oil is used in soaps and fertilizer.

Hazel

HAZEL FLOWERS arrive before the leaves, followed by yellow male catkins and tiny female ones, almost hidden in the buds. Its delicious nuts are set in a woody shell and a cup of leafy bracts. If the tree is coppiced, fresh shoots allow harvesting every few years; if left to grow, trees may reach 12 metres (40 feet) and live for some 80 years, but coppiced hazel can survive for several hundred years. Fritillary, large emerald, small white wave, barred umber and nut-tree tussock caterpillars munch the leaves. Dormice grow plump on the nuts, ready to hibernate, and then, in their spring emergence, snack on the caterpillars. The nuts are enjoyed by squirrels and mice plus woodpeckers, nuthatches, tits, wood pigeons and jays. Coppiced hazel provides shelter for ground-nesting nightingales, nightjars, yellowhammers and willow warblers. As well as growing in hedgerows and scrubland, hazel is often found in the understorey of deciduous forests, where it can play host to several mosses, lichens and fungi.

LATIN NAME *Corylus avellana*

HABITAT
Native to temperate Northern Hemisphere: Europe, parts of North Africa and Western Asia.
Grows in scrub and hedgerows as well as oak, ash or birch woodland understorey.

HISTORY
In medieval times the tree was a fertility symbol. During ancient Roman wedding ceremonies, hazelnut branches served as torches and were said to ensure a long and happy marriage.

MEANINGS
Reconciliation.

SECRETS AND SPECIAL ASSOCIATIONS
During the Iron Age, Europeans believed hazelnuts offered wisdom and inspiration.
A hazel rod was said to protect against evil spirits.
Hazel branches serve for water-divining.
Hazel nuts were carried as charms.
In Irish, Norse and Roman mythology, hazel was known as the 'Tree of Knowledge'.

INTRIGUING INFORMATION
Hazel pollen is slithery so bees find it difficult to collect and can gather only small loads.
Hazel is so bendy in spring that it can be tied in a knot without breaking.
Its wood can be twisted as well as knotted and makes good wattle panelling in walls, fencing, thatching spars, net stakes, hurdles, furniture, baskets and coracle boat frames.
Coppiced hazel provides useful pea sticks and beanpoles.

The best time to plant a tree was twenty years ago. The next best time is now.

Keep a green tree in your heart and perhaps a singing bird will come.

Chinese proverbs

I am a forest, and a night of dark trees: but he who is not afraid
of my darkness, will find banks full of roses under my cypresses.
Friedrich Nietzsche (1844–1900), Germany

Within its gates I heard the sound
Of winds in cypress caverns caught
Of huddling tress that moaned, and sought
To whisper what their roots had found.
George Sterling (1869–1926), USA

Cypress

EVERGREEN WITH needle-like leaves, these soldier-like trees stand to attention some 5–40 metres (16–130 feet) tall. Many species are adapted to surviving forest fires, so hold their seeds for many years in closed cones until the trees are burned, at which point the seeds are released to colonize the bare, scorched earth. Some species are grown as decorative trees in parks and around Asian temples. The Mediterranean cypress (Italian, Tuscan or Persian cypress, black cypress or pencil pine) is very long-lived and may survive well over 1,000 years.

LATIN NAME *Cupressus*
Cupressus sempervirens (Mediterranean cypress)

HABITAT
Native to warm, temperate regions in the
Northern Hemisphere: the Americas,
some Himalayan valleys, southern China,
northern Vietnam, northwest Africa, the
Middle East and the Mediterranean, where
the Mediterranean cypress thrives in eastern
regions including Italy, Libya, Albania,
Croatia, Montenegro, Greece, Turkey,
Cyprus, Egypt, Syria, Lebanon, Malta,
Jordan and Palestine.
It adapts well and survives cooler, wetter regions
but cannot tolerate severe frost.

HISTORY
In ancient Athens, households in mourning
were garlanded with boughs of cypress.
In Provence, France, cypresses were planted
as a windbreak against the mistral winds.
They were also planted in threes outside
farmhouses as a sign of hospitality.

MEANINGS
Death, despair, mourning.

SECRETS AND SPECIAL ASSOCIATIONS
Associated with funerals and cemeteries, and a
symbol of death and immortality.
In Turkey the tree is referred to as the cemetery
tree or black cypress.

INTRIGUING INFORMATION
There is a 4,000-year-old Mediterranean
cypress in Yazd, Iran.
They are sometimes described as 'exclamation
mark' trees.
This durable, scented wood was used for the
doors of St. Peter's Basilica in Rome's Vatican
City.
It has also served as distillery staves, for musical
instruments (flamenco guitars and Italian
harpsichords), furniture, boatbuilding and
turned objects.
In cosmetics its oil acts as an
astringent, fragrance, anti-aging
skin treatment and to
combat dandruff.

Ebony

EBONY IS a multi-branched, spiny, deciduous tree that grows some 20 to 30 metres (65 to 98 feet) tall. Its extensive root system sees it through the long, African dry season. The scaly, grey bark is often covered with mosses and lichens. With its dark heartwood and beautifully smooth finish when polished, jet-black ebony is greatly valued as an ornamental wood. Sadly, ebony has been heavily over-harvested and is now endangered, especially those species in Africa, where trees have all too often been cut down illegally. Giraffes, elephants and rhinos munch the leaves, while warthogs, velvet monkeys and baboons enjoy the fruit.

LATIN NAME *Diospyros*

HABITAT
Native to western Africa, Indonesia, Sri Lanka and southern India.
Ebony is not competitive and prefers a solitary lifestyle in fertile, moist soil in tropical rainforests.

HISTORY
Carved pieces of ebony have been found in ancient Egyptian tombs.
By the end of the 16th century, craftsmen in Antwerp were creating fine ebony cabinets with low-relief carving, a practice adopted by Parisian masters called *ébénistes* (still a French term for a cabinet maker).
In Japan ebony was used for samurai sword handles.

MEANINGS
Blackness

SECRETS AND SPECIAL ASSOCIATIONS

The wood was thought to be resistant to poison; ancient kings of India had drinking cups made of ebony.

INTRIGUING INFORMATION
This is the most expensive, strongest and finest African wood.
Weighing more than 955 kilograms per cubic metre (60 pounds per cubic foot), it is dense and heavy enough to sink in water.
It has been used for musical instruments including clarinets, the black keys on pianos and harpsichords, parts of violins, violas and their bows, mandolins, bagpipes, guitars, double basses and cellos. It is also used for jewellery, handgun grips, pool cue butts, knife handles, fine furniture, black chess pieces and traditional carvings.
It makes good charcoal.
Pure black ebony comes only from trees that are at least 150 years old.
The succulent fruit of Gabon ebony is edible and is also used to make beer, wine and brandy.
The bark is a source of dark blue pigment – used for painting cloth.

Trees are poems that earth writes upon the sky. We fell them down and turn them into paper, that we may record our emptiness.
Kahlil Gibran (1883–1931), Lebanon

Of all man's works of art, a cathedral is greatest. A vast and majestic tree is greater than that.
Henry Ward Beecher (1813–87), USA

Does a dragon still sing from within a withered tree?
Dōgen (1200–53), Japan

God has cared for these trees, saved them from drought, disease, avalanches, and
a thousand tempests and floods. But he cannot save them from fools.
John Muir (1838–1914), Scotland/USA

Dragon Tree

ALSO KNOWN as drago, this rare, slow-growing member of the asparagus family is named after its red resin, called dragon's blood. On the Canary Islands, flowering of all the dragon trees occurs almost simultaneously, only about once every fifteen years when it produces a flower spike with lily-like, white, perfumed flowers, followed by red or coral berries, smaller than a cherry. As the crown of terminal buds appears, the plant starts creating branches that also grow for about ten to fifteen years. At this point they flower and branch out until the mature dragon tree assumes an umbrella-like shape. The most ancient (and largest) specimen is El Drago Milenaria (the 'thousand-year-old dragon') in northwest Tenerife, estimated to be some 300 to 400 years old.

LATIN NAME *Dracaena draco*

HABITAT
Dry forests, mountains or steep inaccessible coastal cliffs.
A few hundred trees are found on five of the seven Canary Islands.
There are two specimens in Madeira and up to 80 on the Azorean Islands, particularly on Ilha das Flores.
In western Morocco and Cape Verde it grows high up the mountains.

MEANINGS
Snare.

SECRETS AND SPECIAL ASSOCIATIONS
In Greek myth, Hercules killed a hundred-headed dragon and as its blood flowed upon the ground, a dragon tree sprang up.
It is thought that a flightless, dodo-like bird may have helped dragon tree seeds to germinate by semi-digesting them. The bird became extinct about 500 years ago.

In Tenerife, the Guanche people worshipped an ancient dragon tree and hollowed out its trunk into a sanctuary.
The Guanche used the sap in their mummification processes when embalming the dead.
It is an official symbol of Tenerife.

INTRIGUING INFORMATION
Dragon's blood was used as an ancient Roman dye.
It has served to stain Stradivarius violins, as incense and to make beehives.
It makes an anti-oxidant for iron tools, and is in varnish, toothpastes, tinctures and plasters.
Goats may munch away at the leaves.

Rainbow Eucalyptus and Eucalyptus

VER 700 species of eucalyptus include gum trees (prevalent in Australia) and the rainbow eucalyptus tree, with its stunningly beautiful bark, from Indonesia and islands north and west of Australia. As the previous season's bark peels off in strips, the rainbow eucalyptus reveals a bright, neon green inner bark that darkens and matures into brightly coloured vertical streaks of red, orange, green, grey, blue and maroon, especially vivid and dramatic when the tree is flourishing in its native habitat. It is thought that the bark-shedding may reduce the invasion of plants and parasites on the trunk. The oil from gum trees can give a blue haze to the air, as in Australia's Blue Mountains.

LATIN NAME *Eucalyptus*
Eucalyptus deglupta (Rainbow eucalyptus)

HABITAT
Most are native to Australia but are now cultivated widely.
Eucalyptus deglupta
Mindanao, New Britain, New Guinea, Suram and Sulawesi; its range extends into the Northern Hemisphere.
It thrives in wet tropical forests in Indonesia and is grown for pulpwood in the Philippines.
It survives (albeit at only half the height) in the USA in frost-free climates such as Hawaii and Florida.

HISTORY
In Hawaii the rainbow trees were planted to help control soil erosion after over-logging.

MEANINGS
Protection.

SECRETS AND SPECIAL ASSOCIATIONS
Eucalyptus is beloved by koala bears, termites and the large bentwing ghost moth.
As the colours of rainbow eucalyptus continuously alter, the trees seem like living kaleidoscopes.

INTRIGUING INFORMATION
Used as an ornamental tree where the climate permits.
Eucalyptus produces an aromatic oil, used for cleaning, antiseptics, deodorizers, cough drops, toothpaste and decongestants.
It may be used for luxury furniture.
Eucalyptus regnans, or the Australian 'mountain ash', is the Earth's tallest known flowering plant at some 99.6 metres (327 feet) high.
Eucalyptus wood is used for didgeridoos, aboriginal Australian wind instruments.
As the rainbow bark colours constantly change, no two trees ever look the same. Usually the colours are vibrant and rich but in some regions the colours assume a more delicate pastel hue. The multicoloured streaks of constantly changing colours may result from varying levels of tannin and chlorophyll.

If you can imagine the one family continuously occupying the
same land for 40,000 years or more, using it not just to sustain
life but as a place of reverence and worship, where every tree, rock
and waterhole had significance, you will get some understanding
of the importance of land to indigenous people.
Tania Major (1981–), Aboriginal Australia

*I frequently tramped eight or ten miles through the deepest
snow to keep an appointment with a beech-tree …*
Henry David Thoreau (1817–62), USA

The trees that are slow to grow bear the best fruit.
Molière, (1622–73), France

Beech

ESCRIBED BY English poet Edmund Spenser as 'the warlike beech', this great tree can reach 50 metres (160 feet) tall and survive some 150–200 years – occasionally up to 500. It has smooth, grey bark and a stately crown of domed, arching branches. Its glossy leaves become warm orange and gold in autumn, and then crinkled copper over the winter months. Male flowers are carried in small, tassel-like catkins. Paired female flowers produce beechnuts, abundant after a hot summer. Beech forests are very dark, screening out rival trees, and some – such as in Romania – are the haunt of brown bears, wolves and lynx. Butterflies flit in more open glades and along woodland rides. Hole-nesting birds and wood-boring insects inhabit beech trunks where the bark supports a variety of fungi, mosses and lichens. Mice, voles, squirrels and birds relish the seeds while truffle fungi thrive beneath.

LATIN NAME *Fagus sylvatica*

HABITAT
France, Belgium, southern England, Ukraine, Romania, Norway, Sweden, Portugal, central Spain, Sicily, Turkey, the Balkans.
In the southern Mediterranean, it grows only in mountain forests above 600 metres (1,969 feet).
Beech constitutes about 10 per cent of French forests.
It enjoys a humid, misty atmosphere, fertile ground and hillsides.
Beech tolerates freezing winters but does not enjoy late spring frosts.

HISTORY
Stone Age families ate beech nuts.

MEANINGS
Prosperity.
Beech is associated with femininity.

SECRETS AND SPECIAL ASSOCIATIONS
This tree forms a symbiotic relationship with a range of fungi; these enhance its uptake of water and soil nutrients.
Fagus was the Celtic god of beech trees.

INTRIGUING INFORMATION
Their overwintering leaves make beech hedges excellent all-year screens – a great habitat for garden birds.
The timber is used for furniture, flooring, tool handles, boatbuilding, piano pinblocks, plywood and turned objects.
It burns well so is good for fuel and for smoking herrings.
The nuts were used to feed pigs, and may be roasted to serve as a coffee substitute.
Copper beeches (*Fagus sylvatica purpurea*) with purple-red foliage make great ornamental trees.

Fig and Banyan

THE COMMON fig (*Ficus carica*) has been cultivated since ancient times. It can thrive in cracks in rocks or on steep ravines, with old specimens creating a large area of dense shade – greatly welcomed by both people and animals when summer heat is intense. Fig fruit has ever been an important food source for wildlife, while humans enjoy the fruit as a snack, baked into cakes, or dried and saved for the winter. Relished in ancient Greek and Roman times, figs spread across nations through the centuries, reaching California during the gold rush. The banyan seed will develop first in the crevice of a host tree or building and then the tree grows roots down towards the ground, ultimately enveloping much of the host tree or edifice. For this reason, some varieties are known as 'strangler figs'. Deep hollows between the banyan buttresses provide secret shelter for many animals.

LATIN NAME *Ficus*
Ficus carica (fig)
Ficus benghalensis (banyan)

HABITAT
The common fig is now grown worldwide, although happiest in the dry and sunny Middle East or Mediterranean.

HISTORY
One of the earliest cultivated plants, the fig may be the first known instance of agriculture. Partially fossilized examples dating to 9400–9200 BCE have been found near Jericho.

MEANINGS
The fig, like the apple tree, is often cited as a contender for the Biblical Tree of Life, the tree of the knowledge of good and evil. In the Bible, the plant is marked as a blessing, a symbol of prosperity, wellbeing and security.

The giant banyan tree symbolizes wisdom, power, calm and longevity (even immortality).

SECRETS AND SPECIAL ASSOCIATIONS
The fig is pollinated by its own special fig wasp.
The banyan tree is one of the most venerated trees in Hinduism as its leaf is said to be the resting place of the god Krishna. In addition, the god Shiva is often shown sitting in silence under the banyan.
Similarly, the sacred fig tree is highly regarded in Buddhism, as the Buddha was sitting under this tree when he attained enlightenment.

INTRIGUING INFORMATION
Fig trees were flourishing when dinosaurs first roamed the planet.
In Assam, India, the aerial roots of *Ficus elastica* trees are trained into landslide prevention nets and bridges.
The banyan is the national tree of India.
Figs are eaten by creatures as varied as elephants, bats, and giant tortoises.

Nothing great is produced suddenly, since not even the grape or the Fig is. If you say to me now that you want a Fig, I will answer to you that it requires time: let it flower first, then put forth fruit, and then ripen.
Epictetus 55–135 CE, Greece

Train up a fig tree in the way it should go, and when you are old sit under the shade of it.
Charles Dickens (1812–70), England

The ash is the first and greatest of all trees,
which spreads its branches over the whole earth.
The *Edda*, Icelandic poems

Ash

TALL AND graceful ash trees often create a domed canopy, their bark covered with lichens and mosses. Growing up to 35 metres (115 feet) tall, they may survive to the grand old age of 500 years – longer if coppiced. Twig tips support spiked clusters of purple flowers, the male and female blossom separated onto different trees or branches. Their winged keys float down, to be dispersed by birds and mammals. Caterpillars of coronet, brick, centre-barred sallow and privet-hawk moths grow plump on ash leaves with attendant butterflies such as the rare high brown fritillary. Leaves are munched by cows, goats and rabbits while bullfinches peck up the seeds. Owls, woodpeckers, redstarts and nuthatches nest in ash trees while down below dog violet, wild garlic, dog's mercury, lesser stag beetles and dormice thrive. European or common ash has been threatened by dieback caused by a fungus (*Hymenoscyphus fraxineus*) and in 2016 was reported in danger of extinction. In North America, the emerald ash borer beetle from eastern Asia has killed millions of trees and threatens millions more.

LATIN NAME *Fraxinus*

HABITAT
Native to Europe, from the Mediterranean to Norway and the Arctic Circle, plus Turkey and western Russia. Now spread worldwide.

HISTORY
Ash and elm were once called 'widow makers' because large boughs may drop without warning and cause fatalities.

MEANINGS
Grandeur and prudence.
Also ambition, sensitivity and awareness.

SECRETS AND SPECIAL ASSOCIATIONS
Ash wood was burned to ward off evil spirits. Its winged seeds are believed to hold the key to universal understanding and knowledge.

INTRIGUING INFORMATION
The leaves follow the sun; sometimes the whole tree crown may lean towards the sunlight.
The ash may change its sex from year to year.
A tough hardwood, ash can absorb shocks without splintering.
It is used for making furniture, tools, hammers, axes, spades, hockey sticks, baseball and softball bats, oars, shafts for bows and arrows, staircases and balusters, guitars and drums.

Honey Locust

ALSO KNOWN as sweet bean, sweet locust and honeyshuck, it is named for the sweet pulp hidden within the tree's pods (although it is also sometimes called thorny locust since both branches and trunks bear long, sharp thorns). Strongly scented, cream flower clusters attract bees and are followed by the long, flat pod fruits. These eventually ripen, turning brown or maroon, with tough, dry, leathery skin that sticks tenaciously to the succulent pulp within. Grazing horses and cattle munch the pod pulp and later excrete the seeds (their hard coat now softened) in droppings that will serve as warm fertilizer, making germination easier. Rabbits, deer, squirrels, foxes, hogs, opossums, raccoons and crows may also eat the pods. Honey locusts grow quickly to about 20–30 metres (66–98 feet) but are relatively short-lived in tree terms – some 100 to 150 years. The leaves turn a glowing gold in autumn.

LATIN NAME *Gleditsia triacanthos*

HABITAT
Central North America and central Texas.
Has become invasive in agricultural regions of
Australia.

HISTORY
Its sweet legume pulp was eaten by Native
Americans.
Cherokees in Tennessee used this wood to
construct their bows.

MEANINGS
Affection beyond the grave.

SECRETS AND SPECIAL ASSOCIATIONS
Dense, thorny thickets provide excellent cover
for animals and birds.

INTRIGUING INFORMATION
The robust trees serve well in parks and along
highways as they resist pollution well.
Their rot-resistant timber is good for
furniture, fences, posts, railings, railway
sleepers, warehouse or shipping pallets and
shipbuilding.
The long, hard thorns have been used as nails.
The dried, roasted and ground seeds make a
good coffee substitute.
The pulp can be fermented to make beer.

BEWARE the pods of the unrelated *black*
locust tree *(Robinia pseudoacacia);* these are
toxic!

A tree laden with fruits always bends low. Humility is a sign of greatness.
Sri Ramakrishna (1836–86), India

That same David Crockett … can wade the Mississippi, leap the Ohio, ride upon a streak of lightning, and slip without a scratch down a honey locust.
David Crockett (1786–1836), USA

*These moments under the shade of the jacaranda trees on
the vicarage lawn were the most pleasant of the trial.*
Nelson Mandela (1918–2013), South Africa

*The jacaranda flames on the air like a ghost,
Like a purer sky some door in the sky has revealed.*
Douglas Stewart (1913–85), New Zealand

Jacaranda

HIS FAST-GROWING, elegant tree has soft, green foliage and large panicles of lavender, funnel- or bell-shaped blooms that completely and gloriously cover its canopy in a show that may last for some two months. This explosion of colour is followed by the ground turning blue as the flowers drift down. Soon fleshy, curved seed pods develop that contain flat, winged seeds – all these glories followed by golden leaves in winter. It enjoys grasslands, wooded ravines and riverbanks but, if introduced to an area, its dense, overhanging crown may screen out other, native plants. It is also known as green ebony tree, black poui, Brazilian rosewood, blue trumpet tree or fern tree.

LATIN NAME *Jacaranda mimosifolia*

HABITAT

South-central South America, Mexico and Central America.

It can tolerate only very brief frosts and thrives best in tropical climates.

It has been introduced to Australia, New Zealand, Africa, USA, Spain, Portugal, Italy, Greece, China, Israel, Malta and Cyprus.

HISTORY

In South America's Mayan culture, the jacaranda was a teaching tree that helped enlightenment.

MEANINGS

In the Guarani language of South America jacaranda means 'fragrant'.

Its blossoms represent rebirth and the wonder of spring.

SECRETS AND SPECIAL ASSOCIATIONS

This tree is associated with an Amazonian moon goddess known for her wise understanding.

INTRIGUING INFORMATION

Jacaranda is a popular choice for lining avenues, squares and parks.

It is often planted on university campuses because of its links with knowledge and wisdom.

'Purple panic' is an Australian term for student stress during examinations, which take place just when the jacaranda blooms; it is sometimes called the 'exam tree'.

The pods are used to decorate Christmas trees and dried arrangements.

In China the leaves are used to make a purple dye.

Its pale grey, cream or pinkish wood is straight-grained, knot-free and sweetly scented. It is used in cabinet making, carpentry, luxury car finishing and – in its green state – for bowl carving and turning.

Pretoria in South Africa, often cloaked in a purple haze of blossom, is called 'the Jacaranda City'.

Walnut

CULTIVATED FOR thousands of years, the walnut is a fast-growing tree that develops a broad canopy but requires full sun to thrive. After the buds stir from winter dormancy, large, compound leaves unfurl, giving off a lemon scent when crushed. The male flowers are slender catkins; female flowers are smaller, often on the branch tips. Wind-blown pollen may fertilize trees over a mile away. Ultimately, its spreading branches will be laden with delicious edible nuts, often stored away for Christmas, if not first foraged by squirrels, turkeys or bears.

LATIN NAME *Juglans*

Juglans regia (common, English or Persian walnut)

Juglans nigra (black walnut)

HABITAT

The common walnut probably originated in southeastern Europe but thrives across Europe and central Asia, through the Middle East into the Himalayas.

It now grows in Japan, China, Canada, California, Mexico and Argentina.

The largest forests are in Kyrgyzstan mountains up to 1,000–2,000 metres (3,000–7,000 feet) high.

Other species are native to Asia and the Americas.

HISTORY

Alexander the Great spread the 'Persian nut' in the 4th century BCE.

The Romans took it to southern Europe, northern Africa, France and Britain.

In the Middle Ages, it was dispersed by merchants travelling along the Silk Road.

Black walnuts are native to eastern North America but English colonists took *Juglans regia* to the Americas in the 17th century.

MEANINGS

Intellect, stratagem.

SECRETS AND SPECIAL ASSOCIATIONS

In rural Serbia, a walnut would be cracked open on Christmas morning. If the nut was good then the coming year would be prosperous. If it was wizened, this was a bad omen.

A walnut resembles the human brain and is said to be excellent brain food!

INTRIGUING INFORMATION

In India walnuts are offered to mother goddess Vaishno Devi and enjoyed at festivals.

The glossy oil is an effective binding medium in oil paints.

Walnut shells clean soft metals, fibreglass, plastics, wood, stone, car and jet engines, electronic circuit boards – and paint, so are good for graffiti removal.

Its timber polishes to a very smooth finish and is much prized for furniture, flooring, carving, turning, veneers, guitars, and pipe organ bodies.

The husks can be used to create rich dyes.

A walnut tree may take the power of any who sleep beneath it.

The Earth is a huge walnut tree.
Bulgarian proverbs

A thing which I regret, and which I will try to remedy some time, is that I have never in my life planted a walnut. Nobody does plant them nowadays – when you see a walnut it is almost invariably an old tree. If you plant a walnut you are planting it for your grandchildren, and who cares a damn for his grandchildren?
George Orwell (1903–50), Britain

Elijah lay down and slept under a juniper tree; and behold, there was an angel touching him, and he said to him, 'Arise, eat.'
The Bible, 1 Kings 19:5

My sister, little Marlinchen,
Gathered together all my bones,
Tied them in a silken handkerchief,
Laid them beneath the juniper-tree
Jacob Grimm (1785–1863) and
Wilhelm Grimm (1786–1859), Germany

Juniper

UNIPERS ARE evergreens that rise up 20–40 metres (66–131 feet), with long, trailing branches showing needles or scale-like leaves. Their cone scales fuse together to create a berry-like structure, containing hard-shelled, aromatic seeds that may be used as a spice. These 'berries' may be brown or orange but generally are a cornflower blue, soft purple or navy. Many caterpillars (including juniper carpet moth, juniper pug and the chestnut-coloured carpet) nibble away at junipers, which also provide dense cover for nesting birds such as the goldcrest, firecrest and black grouse. Song thrush, mistle thrush and ring ouzel eat the berries.

LATIN NAME *Juniperus*

HABITAT
Native to much of the Northern Hemisphere.
About 67 juniper species now grow from the Arctic to tropical Africa, from Pakistan to Tibet, Canada and Central America.
It enjoys dry conditions in pine woodland, moorland, open chalk hills and rocky habitats.
The highest-known juniper forest occurs at 4,900 metres (16,000 feet) in the northern Himalayas – one of Earth's highest tree lines.

HISTORY
Prehistoric families often lived in or near juniper forests, thus gaining shelter plus access to timber for building, utensils and fuel.

MEANINGS
Succour, protection.
Also a symbol of longevity, strength, fitness and fertility.

SECRETS AND SPECIAL ASSOCIATIONS
Juniper seeds germinate better if close to where birds perch and feed. The acid in a bird's digestive system may help them to germinate and, once defecated, to break free of their hard shells.
Recent research suggests that juniper seedlings thrive better when in close proximity to mistletoe.

INTRIGUING INFORMATION
A thriving bonsai juniper tree in Japan is thought to be 1,000 years old.
The berries flavour liqueurs, beer and gin – this spirit's name derived from the Dutch word for juniper, *genever*. Juniper berry sauce is especially good with pheasant, veal, rabbit and venison.
The light gold, aromatic wood is used for carving, turning, pencils and basket-making.
In Scotland, the smoke of burning juniper is used to cleanse, bless and protect homes.
The crushed leaves smell of lemons or apples.
Thought to deter witches, juniper was burnt at Halloween.

Larch

SOARING TO heights that exceed 36 metres (120 feet), larches survive for a good 200 years; one in Dunkeld, Scotland, was planted in 1738. With their thick, impermeable bark and hard wood, larches can resist both freezing conditions and forest fires. Male flowers produce creamy-yellow anthers; female flowers (called larch roses) are clusters of scales in pink, green or white. Its green or purple cones may remain on the tree for years, ultimately turning gun-metal grey or black. Although they are conifers, larches do lose their needles in autumn. This tree services countless caterpillars (including those of the autumnal moth, case-bearer moth, larch pug and common emerald). Red squirrels and birds (citril finch, siskin and lesser redpoll) eat the seeds; capercaillie (wood grouse) munch the needles and cones; buds and immature cones are gorged on by black grouse.

LATIN NAME *Larix*

HABITAT

Native to cooler temperate Northern Hemisphere regions in Europe, Asia and North America.

Larches like cool mountainsides (in the Alps, Carpathians and Pyrenees) up to altitudes of 2,400 metres (7,874 feet).

It is a dominant tree in Siberia and Canada's boreal forests.

HISTORY

Larch was used in pagan cremations.

MEANINGS

Audacity, boldness.

SECRETS AND SPECIAL ASSOCIATIONS

In many Eurasian shamanistic rituals, the World Tree is depicted as a larch.

Fungi associated with larch include *Suillus grevillei* (Greville's bolete or larch bolete) which may transfer information from the tree through a fungal network (*see page 142*).

INTRIGUING INFORMATION

Larch is a waterproof, knot-free, tough, durable wood.

It is good for making yachts, small boats, cladding, wall panelling, posts, fencing, gates, garden furniture, roof shingles and coffins.

Many Vikings sailed in ships made from Siberian larch.

Siberian larch was used for many of Russia's oldest buildings, with some 800-year-old larch edifices still standing.

The city of Venice was raised on some larch core pilings.

Knobbly bark, small needles, fresh spring foliage and autumn colour make larch trees excellent bonsai subjects.

That tree whose leaves are trembling: it is yearning for something.
Diego Hurtado de Mendoza (1503–75) Spain

And the Larch, with all its fibres,
Shivered in the air of morning,
Touched his forehead with its tassels ...
'Take them all, O Hiawatha!'
Henry Wadsworth Longfellow (1807–82), USA

Have you ever noticed a tree standing naked against the sky,
How beautiful it is?
All its branches are outlined, and in its nakedness
There is a poem, there is a song.
Jiddu Krishnamurti (1895–1986), India

Sweet Gum

ESPITE ITS common name, the gum or sap is not actually sweet, but it does smell pleasant and has been used for centuries to treat skin problems, coughs, and ulcers. The tree's genus name, *Liquidambar*, refers to the golden colour of the sap. Also known as American redgum, sapgum, starleaf-gum, bilsted, satin-walnut, star-leaved gum and alligatorwood, this deciduous tree can live to 400 years and grows into a narrow, pyramid shape with deeply-lobed foliage. Its pale green flowers develop into hard, spiky fruit pods. The deeply ridged, cork-like exterior encloses a dark red timber. Glossy, star-shaped leaves turn vivid crimson, orange, gold and purple in a fiery autumn glow. The tree offers cover and food to squirrels, chipmunks, deer, doves, blue jays, cardinals, goldfinches, purple finches and mourning doves, plus luna, gypsy and promethea moths.

LATIN NAME *Liquidambar styraciflua*

HABITAT
Native to southeastern USA, especially the lower Mississippi Valley, southern Mexico, Central America and Brazil.
It is a characteristic plant of cloud forests.
It is now grown in all temperate regions and in parts of Australia.

HISTORY
Sweet gum was brought to Europe in 1681 by the English naturalist John Banister.
The resin used to be exported as a solid in barrels.

MEANINGS
No official meaning but associated with healing, fertility and growth, especially by Native Americans.

SECRETS AND SPECIAL ASSOCIATIONS
The Mayans presented Spanish invaders with this 'sweet-smelling liquid amber which, when lighted in the way shown... diffused an agreeable odour'.
The prickly fruits have nicknames such as space bugs, goblin bombs and bommyknockers.

INTRIGUING INFORMATION
Sweet gum's rounded canopy provides excellent shade and it is a popular ornamental for parks, larger gardens, campuses or streets.
Its handsome, fine-grained hardwood, named satin walnut, is sometimes used as imitation mahogany or ebony.
The resins have been used in chewing gum and soaps as well as food flavouring.
Sap extracts deter yellow fever mosquitoes.

Tulip Tree or Yellow Poplar

USUALLY ABOUT 18–50 metres (59–164 feet) high but just occasionally reaching up to 57 metres (190 feet), some tulip trees are said to have survived nearly 500 years. It is named for its superb, tulip-like flowers that are usually a citrus lemon with a central orange flare, a circlet of stamens like sea anemone tentacles and a scent like cucumbers. Their sweet nectar attracts both honey and bumble bees. Glossy, fluttering leaves gleam in the sunlight, turning butter-yellow or red tan in autumn and munched by caterpillars including those of the tulip tree beauty, eastern tiger swallowtail and promethea moth. Its cones comprise multiple thin scales with winged samaras dispersed by the wind. Deer and rabbits nibble both saplings and seeds. Squirrels, mice, cardinal birds, goldfinch, Carolina chickadee and purple finch also enjoy these fruits. It is sometimes known as tulip poplar, canoewood or white wood.

LATIN NAME *Liriodendron tulipifera*

HABITAT
Native to temperate zones of eastern North America, where it is the tallest hardwood tree.
It is abundant on Lake Erie's southern shore and the Southern Appalachian mountains.
Tulip trees do not tolerate shade.
It was introduced to Europe in the 17th century.

HISTORY
It became extinct in Europe after glacial and arid periods.
The ancient Queens Giant tulip tree in New York's Alley Pond Park is probably the oldest living thing in the city and its tallest measured tree.

MEANINGS
No official meaning but associated with attraction, charm and inviting gifts.

SECRETS AND SPECIAL ASSOCIATIONS
Black morel mushrooms are often associated with tulip trees and thrive beneath them.
Pileated woodpeckers sometimes hide their nests in these tall trees.
Some birds drill holes through the bark to obtain the sap.
Insects trapped in the sticky sap are a bonus for birds.

INTRIGUING INFORMATION
The fine-grained, termite-resistant wood is used for musical instruments, furniture, coffins, veneers, pattern timber and more.
In the USA the timber is known as tulipwood and 'poplar'.
The long, straight trunks were hollowed out to make canoes.
It yields a dark red, strong honey.

Heed not the night, a summer lodge amid the wild is mine,
'Tis shadowed by the tulip-tree, 'tis mantled by the vine
William Cullen Bryant (1794–1878), USA

For in the true nature of things, if we rightly consider, every green tree is far more glorious than if it were made of gold and silver.
Martin Luther (1483–1546), Germany

Fragrant o'er all the western groves
The tall magnolia towers unshaded.
Maria Brooks (1794–1845), USA

Magnolia

NAMED AFTER Pierre Magnol, a 17th-century French botanist, the magnolia's origins are ancient, with the *Magnoliaceae* order dating back 95 million years. It has survived ice ages, mountain formation, continental drift and other climatic assaults. Appearing even before bees had arrived on the scene, the magnolia evolved to invite beetle pollination, offering high-protein pollen but no nectar. Its gorgeous, triumphant flowers may be white, yellow, pink, purple or green and have a 'tropical fruit' aroma. As the plant ages, its grey bark turns scaly. Birds peck up the red-toned, kidney-shaped seeds while giant leopard moths nibble the leaves.

LATIN NAME *Magnolia*

HABITAT
From Southeast Asia and the Americas, but now in almost every continent.

HISTORY
In 7th-century China, magnolias were symbols of purity and were popular temple garden trees.

MEANINGS
In the European language of flowers it means dignity and perseverance.
In China it symbolizes yin (the feminine): womanly beauty, gentleness, purity, dignity and nobility.

SECRETS AND SPECIAL ASSOCIATIONS
The fragrant magnolia is the national flower of North Korea.
In the USA it is associated with the Southern states: Mississippi is nicknamed the Magnolia State and Houston, Texas is named the Magnolia City.
Different beetles pollinate different species.

INTRIGUING INFORMATION
The Aztecs of Mesoamerica cultivated magnolias, including one that is now very rare.
The variety called 'Atlas' boasts the biggest flowers, which can reach 36 centimetres (14 inches) across.
In Asian cuisine, young leaves, petals and buds are eaten – some being pickled to make condiments, flavour rice or scent tea.
In Japan, the leaves serve as cooking dishes and to wrap food.
Referring to his Southern origins, in the 1960s the *New York Post* said that future president Lyndon Johnson '… spoke with a magnolia accent'.

Apple

PPLE WAS once a generic term for all non-berried fruit, including nuts, so its history can be misinterpreted (including possibly Adam and Eve's interest). This tree has delicate, pink and white blossom, beloved of bees, and, as well as cooking apples, produces delicious, sweet fruits from which cider is made, as well as apple cider vinegar which was produced back in ancient Egypt, Greece and Rome. Part of the rose family, apples have been enjoyed since 6500 BCE and appear to have been cultivated in prehistoric times by Swiss lake-dwellers.

LATIN NAME *Malus domestica*

HABITAT
Native to Central Asia and the Middle East; spread around the world.

HISTORY
In the late Neolithic or early Bronze Age, travellers carried the seed of Central Asian wild apples to Persia (Iran) and Greece, either intentionally or in the stomachs of pack animals.

The Romans planted orchards across western Europe from which apples would diversify worldwide over some 2,000 years.

Today there are more than 7,500 known apple cultivars.

MEANINGS
Temptation, preference. Also a symbol for knowledge, immortality, temptation and humanity's fall into sin.

SECRETS AND SPECIAL ASSOCIATIONS
The larynx is dubbed Adam's apple because the forbidden fruit was said to have remained in his throat.

It has been suggested that Isaac Newton understood the effects of gravity after being hit on the head by a falling apple.

The apple is the national fruit of Austria.

Apples have been associated with fertility and have also been seen as the food of the dead.

The Greek hero Hercules journeyed to the Garden of the Hesperides to pick the golden apples from the Tree of Life.

INTRIGUING INFORMATION
Apple wood is good for turning and carving, furniture, tool handles and mallet heads.

The Greek doctor Hippocrates used cider vinegar as an antibiotic and antiseptic in 400 BCE.

It takes about 36 apples to create one gallon of apple cider.

Even if I knew that tomorrow the world would go to pieces, I should still plant my apple tree.
Martin Luther (1483–1546), Germany

The best apple is eaten by the bear.
Turkish proverb

Adam ate the apple, and our teeth still ache.
Hungarian proverb

*With time and patience the mulberry leaf becomes a
silk gown.*
Chinese proverb

*Here we go round the mulberry bush,
The mulberry bush, the mulberry bush,
Here we go round the mulberry bush
On a cold and frosty morning.*
Traditional rhyme, 19th-century Britain with parallels
in Scandinavia and the Netherlands

Mulberry

ULBERRIES ARE fast growing when young, but their pace soon slows. Red mulberry trees may reach 21 metres (70 feet) and survive about 75 years. The black counterpart reaches only 9 metres (30 feet), but may produce fruit for hundreds of years, while white mulberries grow 10–20 metres (32-65 feet) tall and live for some seven decades although a few specimens reach 250 years. The white mulberry is widely cultivated to feed silkworms, an industry that was launched in China over 4,000 years ago. Helpful birds relish the fruit and then excrete the seeds elsewhere. Moths such as the common emerald, sycamore and lime hawk-moth crop the plant.

LATIN NAME *Morus*
M. alba (white mulberry)
M. nigra (black mulberry)
M. rubra (red mulberry)

HABITAT
Originally from Mesopotamia, Persia and
  China.
Spread to Europe, Ukraine, Africa and America.

HISTORY
In 1607, European colonists in Virginia noted
  the abundance of mulberry trees and how
  their fruit was eaten by Powhatan tribes.
In the 1600s, England's King James I imported
  10,000 *black* mulberry trees to start an
  English silk weaving industry but silk worms
  feed only on the leaves of the *white* mulberry!

MEANINGS
Wisdom.

SECRETS AND SPECIAL ASSOCIATIONS
In German folklore, mulberry tree roots are
  used by the devil to polish his boots.

INTRIGUING INFORMATION
White mulberries can catapult pollen at
  560 km (350 miles) per hour – over half the
  speed of sound!
The branches are used to make baskets.
Buddhist monks made paper for books from
  mulberry bark.
Vincent van Gogh featured the tree in several
  paintings, including *Mulberry Tree* in 1889.
Although male mulberry plants can irritate
  hayfever sufferers with their copious pollen,
  the female plants absorb dust and pollen
  from the atmosphere.
Dry mulberry wood is used for smoking meats.

Olive

UMANS HAVE been cultivating olives for some 8,000 years, originally in ancient Persia and Mesopotamia. Now some 865 million olive trees flourish worldwide. They grow very slowly and remain squat, but their gnarled and twisted trunks attain great girth. Specimens in Crete and Sardinia may be up to 4,000 years old; several in Jerusalem's Garden of Gethsemane could date back to the time when Jesus walked there. The trees exhibit clusters of small, feathery, white flowers and shimmering, silver-backed foliage but are mainly prized for their green, brown or purple-black fruit – eaten raw, pickled or pressed to produce rich oil.

LATIN NAME *Olea europaea*

HABITAT
Flourishes in environments with hot summers and mild winters – the Mediterranean, Iran, Ethiopia, South Africa, Iraq, California, Hawaii, Florida, Bermuda, Saudi Arabia, Java, Argentina, Chile, Australia and New Zealand.

HISTORY
Fossilized olive leaves on Santorini hail from 37,000 years ago.

In 3000 BCE, olives were grown commercially in Crete and may have been the source of Minoan wealth.

Olives appear in the Bible, Greek mythology and ancient Egyptian art.

In ancient Greece olives were sacrificial offerings; the Olympic Games 'eternal flame' was fuelled by olive oil.

Spanish colonists brought olives to Chile and Peru.

MEANINGS
Peace.

It also symbolizes wisdom, glory, fertility, power and purity.

SECRETS AND SPECIAL ASSOCIATIONS
Legends claim that olive trees were created by the Greek goddess Athena as a gift to the city that bears her name.

Officers of the Spanish Inquisition thought that cooking with olive oil rather than lard suggested a secret Jewish faith.

Olympic Games victors were crowned with olive leaves.

The dove brought Noah an olive leaf, showing that the flood and God's anger were over.

The United Nations has two olive branches on its flag.

INTRIGUING INFORMATION
Olives provide oil for lighting, as in ancient Greek temple lamps.

Leafy olive branches were found in pharaoh Tutankhamun's tomb.

Most harvested olives – 90 per cent – are turned into oil. A single tree may produce up to 20 gallons of oil each year.

Take oil of olive and massage with it – it is a blessed tree.
Muhammad (570–632), Arabia

He too, while the olive trees trembled in the fierce breath of the Infinite, had brushed away the fearful cup that appeared before him …
Victor Hugo (1802–85), France

Like a twisted olive tree in its 500th year, giving then its finest fruit, is man. How can he give forth wisdom until he has been crushed and turned in the Hand of God.
Rabbi Akiva (*c.*50–135), Judea (Israel)

It is good to know the truth, but it is better to speak of palm trees.
Arab proverb

Mock the palm tree only when the date harvest is over.
Ethiopian saying

*The palm-tree grows best beneath a ponderous weight, even so the
character of man.*
Lajos Kossuth (1802–94), Hungary

Date Palm

FOSSIL RECORDS suggest that the date palm has existed for some 50 million years. Its trunk, scarred with diamond-shaped leaf bases, rises to a crown of graceful, shimmering, feather-like leaf fronds, its lower leaves curving towards the ground. Floral spikes form on branch leaf axils, with male and female flowers on separate plants, pollinated by wind and insects. More than 1,000 dates may create a single cluster. The tree grows about 23 metres (75 feet) tall and may live for 150 years.

LATIN NAME *Phoenix dactylifera*

HABITAT

Native to North Africa's Sahara and the Middle East (mainly Iraq).

Now also grows in the Canary Islands, north Mediterranean, south USA, south Asia.

Prefers semi-arid habitats near water sources in deserts, swamps and mangrove coasts.

HISTORY

Cultivated in ancient Mesopotamia, prehistoric Egypt and Neolithic Pakistan.

Palms were grown in Roman courtyards and are depicted on frescoes in Pompeii.

Spanish missionaries took date palms to the New World.

MEANINGS

Victory.

The word date comes from the Greek word *daktylos*, meaning finger.

In Egyptian hieroglyphics a full date palm represented a year.

Palm fronds symbolized victory in Roman triumphal processions.

SECRETS AND SPECIAL ASSOCIATIONS

During Muslims' Ramadan fasting, a date is the traditional first food after sunset.

Christians celebrate Palm Sunday to mark Christ's triumphal entry into Jerusalem.

At the Jewish Feast of the Tabernacle, palm, willow and myrtle branches are bound with dried palm leaves.

The date palm is the Middle Eastern Tree of Life, and the national symbol of Saudi Arabia and Israel.

INTRIGUING INFORMATION

Palm tree parts make items as varied as basketry, rope, mattress stuffing, fans, fuel, beehives and shelters.

Seeds are ground for stock feed (good for camels) or as a coffee additive.

Fruit and sap make vinegar, syrup, alcohol, liqueur, palm wine and jaggery (sugar).

Stripped fruit clusters serve as brooms.

On desert treks, dates were a main source of nourishment for nomads.

Some scholars believe a date – not an apple – tempted Eve in the Garden of Eden.

Spruce

A WHORL OF spiralling branches, ranging from silvery-green to blue-green, create the tree's elegant cone shape. Each needle clings to a small 'peg' that remains after the needles tumble off. Norway spruce trees serve as splendid Christmas trees with Oslo presenting magnificent annual specimens for the central squares of London, Edinburgh and Washington DC. Spruce seeds are munched by voles, shrews, mice, squirrels, chipmunks and birds like crossbills, tree creepers, coal tits, warblers and nuthatches. Caterpillars, porcupines, deer and rabbits also nibble on parts of the tree, while black bears strip bark off white spruce.

LATIN NAME *Picea*

HABITAT
Temperate zones in northern, central and
    eastern Europe.
Also China, Japan, North America and Mexico.

HISTORY
The roots of Old Tjikko, a Norway spruce in
    Sweden, are 9,558 years old, making it the
    world's third oldest tree, all of them clonal
    rather than individual trees.
British explorer Captain James Cook used
    fresh spruce shoots to make an alcoholic
    drink, rich in vitamin C, to prevent his crew
    suffering scurvy.
Norway spruce provided massive masts for
    sailing ships.
Spruce was used in some Viking longships.
    The Wright Brothers used
    spruce timber to build their
    first aircraft.

MEANINGS
    Native American meaning:
    peace.

Also a mother's protection, ancient wisdom,
    purification, spiritual refreshment, energy,
    healing.
In Bavaria, it is a symbol of life; its trunk often
    served as a maypole.
The word 'spruce' derives from the French
    pruce, meaning Prussia – thought to be the
    original home of these trees.

SECRETS AND SPECIAL ASSOCIATIONS
Leaves of spruce, oak and beech are said to
    register 'pain' when chewed and send out
    electrical signals that spur on the production
    of chemical defences.
Birds roost in their sheltering branches over
    winter.

INTRIGUING INFORMATION
Stradivarius violins used spruce tonewood as do
    guitars, mandolins, cellos, pianos and harps.
Native Americans wove the slim, pliable roots
    into baskets and used them to sew together
    bark for canoes.
Sculptures, furniture, paper, bridges, mining
    timbers and beer have been made from
    spruce.
Its resin served to make pitch.

'Listen to the trees talking in their sleep,' she whispered, as he lifted her
to the ground. 'What nice dreams they must have!'
L.M. Montgomery (1874–1942), Canada

Thousands of lights were burning on the green branches … The lights
of the Christmas tree rose higher and higher, she saw them now as stars
in heaven; one fell down and formed a long trail of fire.
Hans Christian Andersen (1805–75), Denmark

In snowbound, voiceless mountain depths, to herald
spring, pine trees sound in tune.
Princess Shikishi (1149–1201), Japan

The pine tree seems to listen, the fir tree to wait: and both
without impatience ...
Friedrich Nietzsche (1844–1900), Germany

Pine

T HE MAJESTIC, fragrant and sun-loving pine is the world's most common coniferous tree, with 100 species thriving in vast forests and surrounding sunlit glades. The most ancient non-clonal living thing may be a Californian bristlecone pine said to be 4,600 years old; the oldest one ever recorded (at least 4,862 years, in Nevada, USA) was accidentally felled in 1964. The smallest include Siberian dwarf pines and the tallest are ponderosa pines at up to 81 metres (268 feet). Pines have thick, protective, flaky bark, candle-like spring shoots, thin pointed needles, scaly spiral cones and seeds relished by grouse, crossbills, jays, nuthatches, siskins, woodpeckers and squirrels.

LATIN NAME *Pinus*

HABITAT
Primarily Northern Hemisphere.
The Sumatran pine is the only one to survive south of the equator.
North American species occur from 12 degrees up to 66 degrees north.

HISTORY
When French explorer Jacques Cartier's ship was trapped in ice near Quebec, a Native Canadian chieftain brewed pine tea for the crew; thus the sailors escaped scurvy – and possibly death.

MEANINGS
Pity, hope.
Native American meaning: wisdom, longevity, peace.

SECRETS AND SPECIAL ASSOCIATIONS
Pinecones may stay on the trees for ten years, the seeds protected under the scales from bad weather and hungry creatures. Then, when conditions are perfect, the scales open and the seeds drift away.
Jack pines regenerate during forest fires; the cones pop open in the heat to distribute seeds just when the fire's devastation has made more light available.

INTRIGUING INFORMATION
Flour can be made from its inner bark.
Its edible seeds are good with salads.
Pine is used for buildings, floors, window frames, furniture, wood pulp, canoes – and coffins.
The cones make festive decorations.
Pine needles work as scented mattress- and pillow-fillers.
Its resin is good for glues, turpentine and waterproofing, being used to seal boats.
Colonial American settlers used hardened pine resin to fill teeth.
Pine pollen is used in Korea for baking.

Plane

FTEN SEEN in city streets, plane trees help remove pollutants. They rise some 20–30 metres (66–98 feet) and occasionally twice that height. The pale, grey-green bark is smooth and shedding or mottled and scaly; older, browner trunks may thicken and crack. The bark breaks off in large flakes as the tree cleanses away pollutants, leaving patchy patterns of grey, green, yellow, white and tan on the inner bark. Its five-pointed, maple-like leaves are sleek and shiny so city grime is soon rained away. In winter, fruit clusters slowly release numerous seeds. The buttonwood variant is North America's largest native broadleaf tree and may divide into several secondary trunks.

LATIN NAME *Platanus* (plane)
Platanus occidentalis (buttonwood or American sycamore)

HABITAT

Native to Iran, planes were imported to ancient Rome and now occupy urban habitats throughout the world, especially London, New York, Sydney, Melbourne and Adelaide.
Buttonwoods are native to eastern North America but now also grow in Australia, Argentina and Europe.

HISTORY

It is thought that the Trojan Horse may have been carved from plane timber.
Gauls honoured plane trees with red wine.
Marco Polo reported a solitary Dry Tree (marking the battle site of Alexander the Great and Darius III in Persia) that may have been a plane.
Napoleon Bonaparte is said to have ordered French roads to be lined with plane trees, so that his soldiers could march in the shade.

MEANINGS

Genius.
It is sometimes called the buttonball tree.

SECRETS AND SPECIAL ASSOCIATIONS

The first camouflage fabric, designed between 1937 and 1942 to disguise uniforms and combat shelters, was inspired by plane tree patterns.
Vincent van Gogh enjoyed painting under their shade.

INTRIGUING INFORMATION

Its quarter-sawn timber is highly decorative and flecked, and is one of many called lacewood because its patterns look like delicate lace.
It is good for carpentry and cabinet making.
The London plane (probably a hybrid of buttonwood and Oriental plane) accounts for over half of that city's tree population.
Buttonwood is so-called because it was often used to make buttons.

The chestnut's proud, and the lilac's pretty,
The poplar's gentle and tall,
But the plane tree's kind to the poor dull city –
I love him best of all.
Edith Nesbit (1858–1924), England

In a forest of a hundred thousand trees, no two leaves are alike.
And no two journeys along the same path are alike.
Paulo Coelho (1947–), Brazil

Whoever sees the sky reflected in water, also sees fish in the trees.
Chinese proverb

Poplar

HE POPLAR tree family includes grey and white poplars as well as black poplar (cottonwood) and trembling aspen, *Populus tremuloides*. Also known as quaking aspen, American aspen, quakies, mountain or golden aspen, white poplar or popple, this is the most widespread tree in North America. Tall trembling aspens may live for only about 50 years but in warmer areas swiftly shoot up to 25 meters (82 feet) high, presenting smooth, pale bark, scarred with black lenticels. Older trunks may be deeply ridged. Brilliant, glossy green leaves flutter in the wind (earning the tree its name of 'quaking aspen') and then turn a glowing, golden yellow in autumn. Early flowers mutate into dangling catkins. Deer and moose enjoy the tree's shade while elk delight in stripping off its bark with their front teeth. Ruffed grouse may depend on quaking aspens for food and nesting habitats.

LATIN NAME *Populus*
Populus tremuloides (Trembling aspen)

HABITAT
Throughout the Northern Hemisphere, mostly in temperate climates and often near rivers, ponds and swampy areas.
Populus tremuloides thrives in cooler North America, from Canada to central Mexico.

HISTORY
Greeks, Etruscans and medieval weapon-makers made light shields from European poplar.
During the 6th century, Romans planted poplars in areas where public meetings were held. The Latin name for 'people' is *populus*, hence the name of the tree.

MEANINGS
In Ukrainian folklore poplars symbolize beauty or the loneliness of a woman in love.
The poplar denotes emotion and sorrow.

SECRETS AND SPECIAL ASSOCIATIONS
In Greek mythology the white poplar was consecrated to the hero Hercules because he destroyed a giant near a poplar-covered hill. Greek heroes wore poplar garlands in battle.

INTRIGUING INFORMATION
Poplar wood is soft so is used for Camembert cheese boxes.
Quaking aspen wood is used in pulp for books, newsprint and fine printing paper.
Because they grow fast, poplars are useful as repopulators of disturbed areas, for example after a volcanic eruption.
Leonardo da Vinci's *Mona Lisa* was painted on a poplar panel.
Some aspen groves share a root system. An entire stand of what appear to be individual trees may be, in fact, a clone of multiple stems that form a single, genetic individual. Then all the trees will change leaf color at the same time in autumn. The entire clone may survive for tens of thousands of years.

Plum and Cherry

IKE OTHER stone fruit trees, plums and cherries belong to the *Prunus* genus. In China plum blossom symbolizes resilience and perseverance in the face of adversity because, not only may these trees bloom most vibrantly amid the harsh winter snows, but they can also prove long-lived, ancient trees with wonderful, bent, twisting branches. The wild cherry tree is native to most of Europe and cherries have been enjoyed for thousands of years, but the sweet cherry was a later arrival than the plum; it was spread by the Romans and then reintroduced elsewhere.

LATIN NAME *Prunus*
Prunus domestica (European plum)
Prunus salicina (Chinese or Japanese plum)
Prunus avium (sweet or wild cherry)

HABITAT
Grown on every continent bar Antarctica. All flourish best in sheltered orchards.

HISTORY
Plums may have been one of the first fruits domesticated; their remains have been found in Neolithic archaeological sites.
Prunes (dried plums) were a staple food of the Tartars, Mongols, Turks and Huns.
The Romans probably discovered cherries in Asia Minor around 70 BCE.
In England, King Henry VIII's fruiterer introduced the sweet cherry tree.

MEANINGS
Both trees are linked to endurance and vitality.
Cherry tree: good education.
Cherry tree in winter: deception.
Plum tree: fidelity. Blossom: beauty and longevity.
Indian plum: privation.

SECRETS AND SPECIAL ASSOCIATIONS
Prunus trees 'test' the temperature before flowering to avoid frost damage.
The flowering times may indicate climate change.
Certain rodents and birds like the hawfinch can crack open the stones to eat the kernel inside.

INTRIGUING INFORMATION
Plum
Dried and pickled plums are enjoyed in Asia.
Good plum wine tastes like port. In the Balkans, plums are made into slivovitz brandy.
Cherry
The Japanese enjoy cherry blossom ice cream.
Cherry wood is used for musical instruments.
The German for cherry liqueur, Kirsch, comes from 'karshu' – the cherries first cultivated in Mesopotamia in 8 BCE.
Prunus tree blossom is much celebrated in Japan and America.

Let us learn to appreciate there will be times when the trees
will be bare, and look forward to the time when we may pick
the fruit.
Anton Chekhov (1860–1904), Russia

If you want to know the taste of a pear, you must change the pear by eating it.
Mao Zedong (1893–1976), China

After stuffing pears within, drink old wine until they swim.
Spanish proverb

The best pears fall into the pigs' mouths.
Italian proverb

Pear

GLISTENING WHITE flowers are followed by bulbous, sweet fruits enjoyed since prehistoric days and described for over 3,000 years in China – from whence they spread along mountain chains to temperate zones. The Romans ate them raw or cooked (Pliny recommended stewing them with honey). Asian varieties have a crispy texture and firm consistency; European pears become soft and juicy as they ripen. Pears were sacred to the Greek goddesses Hera and Aphrodite (and their Roman equivalents, Juno and Venus), as well as to Pomona, goddess of fruitfulness.

LATIN NAME *Pyrus*

HABITAT
Native to western China and the Caspian shores; spread to Europe in ancient times. Now grown in temperate zones worldwide.

HISTORY
Around 2500 BCE pears were domesticated in Asia.
The Greek poet Homer, flourishing around the 9th century BCE, recorded pears in Europe.
By around 850 BCE pears were important cultivars in France.

MEANINGS
European meanings: affection, comfort.
In ancient China pears symbolized immortality.

SECRETS AND SPECIAL ASSOCIATIONS
Mural paintings long hidden at Pompeii show both the pear tree and its fruit.

INTRIGUING INFORMATION
Pear wood is good for carving, furniture, woodwind instruments, piano keys, violin and guitar fingerboards, veneers, spoons, scoops, umbrella handles and measuring instruments.
Rulers for architects are made from pear because the wood does not warp.
Pear's aromatic firewood smokes meat well.
Some 3,000 known varieties of pears are grown worldwide.
Fermented pears make perry cider, as the Romans well knew; they took the drink with them across Europe.

Oak

HE USUAL lifespan of an oak is about 200 years but some ancient specimens have survived over 1,200 years. Native to the Northern Hemisphere, there are about 600 oak species. These huge, majestic trees can reach 21 metres (70 feet) high and nearly 3 metres (9 feet) wide. Oaks are home to hundreds of insects and countless birds, while forest creatures – such as deer, ducks, pigs, badgers, squirrels, mice and pigeons – forage for the acorns, which are also used for making flour or coffee. Mushrooms and toadstools flourish in oak trees' basal shade while truffles such as the black Périgord enjoy symbiotic relationships with these mighty neighbours.

LATIN NAME *Quercus*

HABITAT
Oaks range from Mediterranean semi-desert to subtropical rainforests.
North America boasts 90 species; Mexico has 160 (with 109 endemic or only found there); China proffers about 100.
They are vital components of hardwood forests.

HISTORY
In Republican Rome anyone who saved a citizen's life in war was given an oak-leaf crown.
Oak planks were used for Viking longships.
After the Battle of Worcester in 1651, the future Charles II of England hid in an oak tree to escape Roundhead soldiers. His birthday, 29 May, was celebrated as Oak Apple Day from 1660 until 1859.
In 1863, the Emancipation Proclamation was first read to African Americans of the Southern USA under the 'Emancipation Oak' at Hampton University (one of the 10 Great Trees of the World according to the National Geographic Society).

MEANINGS
Strength and endurance, steadfastness, stability.
The symbol of an 80th wedding anniversary.

SECRETS AND SPECIAL ASSOCIATIONS
Tree of the Norse and Finnish thunder gods, Thor and Jumala.
Oaks were sacred to the druids.
Oak is the national tree of countries as varied as the USA, France, Germany and Poland.

INTRIGUING INFORMATION
Oaks are more likely to be struck by lightning than other trees.
An English oak can support 284 insect species.
Strong oak timber is used to make ships, furniture, floors, wall panels and barrels.
The tannin-rich bark serves in leather making and for roof shingles.

Great oaks from little acorns grow.
14th-century proverb

*At the edge of the road stood an oak … It was an enormous
tree, its girth twice as great as a man could embrace …
scowling, rigid, misshapen, and grim.*
Leo Tolstoy (1828–1910), Russia

On the fall of an oak, every man gathers wood.
Meander of Athens (342 BCE–292 BCE), Ancient Greece

The wonder is that we can see these trees and not wonder more.
Ralph Waldo Emerson (1803–82), USA

Black Locust

AMED FOR its dark bark, these trees have zigzag, prickly branches and pods that hang on the branches until early spring, attracting birds and small mammals like squirrels. Later, dangling pendants of fragrant, pea-like flowers – mostly white or sometimes pink – offer copious nectar relished by so many bees that the air actually hums. This is a major honey plant in the USA, a source of the famed acacia honey. Bobwhite quail eat the seeds, although the leaves, bark and wood are poisonous. The tree's extremely hard, rot-resistant timber is much prized and it was once dubbed 'shipmast locust' because of its valuable, long, straight trunk. It tolerates pollution well and so is often planted in city parks and streets.

LATIN NAME *Robinia pseudoacacia*

HABITAT

Black locust grows mainly in the eastern United States, especially prairie and savanna regions of the Midwest, where it may displace grasses, and on the lower slopes of the Appalachian Mountains. The trees love open sunshine. They enrich sandy soils, fixing nitrogen and acting as a primary colonizer after natural disasters.

They have spread to Canada, South America, Europe, Australia, New Zealand, China, India, Pakistan, North and South Africa.

HISTORY

The name 'locust' is said to have been given by Jesuit missionaries, who wrongly thought St. John ate its pods in the wilderness.

Its Latin name might derive from plantsman Jean Robin (or his son Vespasien), gardeners to Henry IV of France, who, in the early 1600s introduced the tree to France.

MEANINGS

Elegance.

SECRETS AND SPECIAL ASSOCIATIONS

It emits an amazing yellow-green fluorescence, visible under black light.

It is thought to repel mosquitoes.

Woodpeckers may hide their nests in its hollowed trunks.

INTRIGUING INFORMATION

Horses that consume its toxic leaves or bark may develop anorexia, depression and irregular heartbeat.

However, heating destroys the poison and its leaves can be turned into livestock feed in Korea and Bulgaria.

The strong wood expands when wet and becomes leak-proof, so it was used for ships' nails that often lasted longer than the hulls they pinned.

European pioneers in North America built ships and houses with black locust wood.

Its tough heartwood can last over a century in the soil as fence posts.

Willow

WILLOW BRANCHES rise from a massive root system that vigorously seeks out water. Tiny, yellow, spring flowers produce male and female catkins on separate trees. Willow branches are flexible and have served to create many a wicker basket. Some Welsh coracles had willow frameworks and the oldest known fishing net, found in Finland dating to 8300 BCE, was also made from willow. The mourning cloak butterfly is a regular visitor, as are wasps, while wood ants march up willow trunks to collect aphid honeydew. There are about 400 species of willow: broader-leaved ones are sometimes called sallows, and narrow-leaved ones osiers, while the weeping willow is much loved for its graceful foliage.

LATIN NAME *Salix*

Salix × sepulcralis (weeping willow, a hybrid of Peking willow *S. babylonica* and white willow *S. alba*)

HABITAT

Cold and temperate Northern Hemisphere.
All relish moist soils along stream banks or lake shores.

HISTORY

Weeping willows originated in China, reached Europe via Southwest Asia and the Middle East by 1730, and then crossed to the American colonies.

MEANINGS

Mourning, grief, sadness and sorrow.
In the 19th century, British and American mourning clothes were often embroidered with a weeping willow motif. Conversely, to the Arapahoe Native Americans willow symbolized longevity.

SECRETS AND SPECIAL ASSOCIATIONS

Claude Monet painted a series of Weeping Willow tree scenes to honour French soldiers who fell during World War I.

It tolerates sulphur dioxide, preventing water and soil erosion or contamination.

The tree is associated with fertility, mysticism and witchcraft.

Witches' brooms were said to be made from willow tree twigs.

INTRIGUING INFORMATION

Used for baseball and cricket bats, doors, boxes, floors, baskets, fish traps, fences, wattle and daub, brooms, dolls, toys, three-dimensional sculptures, flutes, whistles, double bass parts, paper, rope and wands.

Willow is a popular material for wicker-work, furniture woven from canes.

The willow tree plays the water like a harp.
Ramón Gómez de la Serna (1888–1963), Spain

The willow which bends to the tempest, often escapes better than the oak which resists it …
Albert Schweitzer (1875–1965), France/Germany

Do behold the King in his glory, King Sequoia! Behold! Behold!
John Muir (1838–1914), Scotland/USA

Though a tree grows so high, the falling leaves return to the root.
Proverb from Malayasia

Redwood or Sequoia

A
LSO KNOWN as the giant redwood, Sierra redwood or Wellingtonia, this is the world's most massive tree by volume, reaching a majestic 50–85 metres (164–279 feet) tall and 6–8 metres (20–26 feet) diameter. Occasionally one may top 94.8 metres (311 feet); the largest are like 26-storey skyscrapers. It should not be confused with the coastal redwood (*Sequoia sempervirens*), which is even taller. Scant resin and pitch plus thick, fibrous bark help giant sequoia survive forest fires and many carry the scars to prove it. Their cones are liberated when dried by fire – which also clears competing vegetation and allows sunlight through, helping seedlings survive. Moreover, trees may sprout afresh from their boles if branches are burned or broken.

LATIN NAME *Sequoiadendron giganteum*

HABITAT

Widely distributed in prehistoric times (until the last ice age) through North America, Eurasia and even China, New Zealand and Australia.

More recently giant sequoia grew naturally only in the Sierra Nevadas, California. Many there are now in national parks.

They relish a humid climate, dry summers, snowy winters and mountainsides of around 1,500–2,100 metres (5,000–7,000 feet).

HISTORY

They are among Earth's most ancient living things; one ring count suggested a 3,500-year existence.

In 1853 giant sequoia seeds were brought to Europe and distributed around the continent.

They also now grow further north in America, including the northeast, and in Australia and New Zealand.

MEANINGS

Symbolizes valour, eternity, enlightenment.

SECRETS AND SPECIAL ASSOCIATIONS

Longhorn beetles lay eggs on the cones; as the larvae bore holes, the cones dry and open so the seeds drop.

Douglas squirrels gnaw on younger cones, thus dislodging a few precious seeds that tumble to the ground.

Tannic acid protects the seeds from rot and insects.

Their bark can be nearly a metre (3 feet) thick.

INTRIGUING INFORMATION

Mature trees may be over 2,200 years old.

A large tree may bear some 11,000 cones.

The world's largest single stem tree by volume (1,487 cubic metres or 52,508 cubic feet) is 2,100-year-old sequoia General Sherman with branches 2.1 metres (6.8 feet) in diameter.

Mahogany

*T*HIS FRAGRANT tree has furrowed and dark grey bark; young leaves are blood-red, quickly turning a bright, light green, then gradually darkening. Mahogany's tiny, light green, star-shaped flowers bloom in clusters, attracting insects such as moths and bees. The resulting 'sky fruits' protrude vigorously upwards (appropriate – as the flowers are used to improve male virility). Later, a woody capsule develops, containing numerous winged seeds. The 18th-century British naturalist Mark Catesby wrote of the wood's resilience: '… excelling Oak, and all other Wood, viz. Durableness, resisting Gunshots …' There are only three genuine *Swietenia* mahogany species, although several other trees – or their lumber – are often known as mahogany.

LATIN NAME *Swietenia macrophylla*
(Honduran or big-leaf mahogany)
S. mahagoni (West Indian or Cuban mahogany)
S. humilis (Pacific Coast mahogany)

HABITAT
Native to the American neotropics from Florida and the Caribbean to Mexico, Central America and Bolivia.
Now grown in plantations in Fiji, Indonesia, India and Bangladesh.

HISTORY
The oldest church in the West Indies, dating to 1514 or earlier, is richly ornamented with carved mahogany.
In the 16th century, mahogany served in the construction, decoration and furnishing of Philip II's El Escorial palace in Madrid, Spain.

MEANINGS
Represents strength, spiritual growth and guidance.
Its Latin name honours the 18th-century Dutch-Austrian physician, Gerard van Swieten.

SECRETS AND SPECIAL ASSOCIATIONS
Mahogany is the national tree of the Dominican Republic and Belize.
Spanish explorers used the timber to make canoes, masts and galleons.
It served in small World War II vessels such as *PT-109*, commanded by John F. Kennedy, which stayed afloat for twelve hours after being rammed.

INTRIGUING INFORMATION
The wood is popular for furniture, panelling and pianos.
Some mahogany trees offer beautifully patterned, 'quilted' wood that is sought after for guitars.
As a 17th-century historian wrote, a mahogany plank is big enough 'that there needs but one to make a large table.'

All our wisdom is stored in the trees.
Santosh Kalwar (1982–), Nepal

A woman is like mahogany: the older she is, the better she is.
Italian proverb

What did the tree learn from the earth to be able to talk with the sky?
Pablo Neruda (1904–73), Chile

*A tree is a wonderful living organism which gives shelter, food,
warmth and protection to all living things. It even gives shade to
those who wield an axe to cut it down.*
Gautama Buddha (*c.*6th–4th century BCE), India

*Slips of yew
Sliver'd in the moon's eclipse.*
William Shakespeare (1564–1616), England

Yew

NOW KNOWN as English or European yew, this evergreen lives longer than any other tree in northern Europe and may survive over 3,000 years. It grows 10–20 metres (33–66 feet) tall, with thin, flaky, purple-tinged bark. The cone contains a single seed, which develops into a red, sweet, juicy, berry-like aril often consumed (and thus dispersed) by waxwings, thrushes, finches, blackbirds, fieldfare and great tits – this digestion weakens the seed's coat, encouraging it to sprout. Squirrels and dormice also munch the aril while satin beauty moth caterpillars feast on the leaves and small birds like goldcrest and firecrest nest in its branches. All yew parts are highly toxic to humans, especially the leaves, and can cause fatal cardiac arrest.

LATIN NAME *Taxus baccata*

HABITAT
Europe, northwest Africa, Iran and Southwest Asia.
Yew often forms the understory in beech woodland.

HISTORY
Yew is the most ancient tree species in Europe.
A yew spearhead found in 1911 in Essex, England may be about 450,000 years old.
Julius Caesar described how an Eburones chief in Gaul (France) poisoned himself with yew rather than submit to Rome.
In 1423 the king of Poland banned the export of yew wood for longbows, a trade that had nearly wiped out the tree in Poland.
Yews were sometimes planted in the cloisters of medieval European monasteries.

MEANINGS
Sorrow, immortality, an omen of doom.

SECRETS AND SPECIAL ASSOCIATIONS
Yew trees may have been planted on the graves of plague victims for protection and purification.
The Romans believed yews grew in hell.
Norsemen and Celts thought yew prevented bewitchment and death; Christians believed its poison protected the dead.
Its branches were carried on Palm Sunday and at funerals.

INTRIGUING INFORMATION
Used for turning, tool handles and longbows.
It is a popular hedging and topiary plant.
Yew is sometimes grown near privies because its scent keeps insects away.
Once a prime choice for lutes, today it is used in guitars.
In Ireland, wine barrels were sometimes made with yew staves, but the Roman naturalist Pliny the Elder stated in his more cautionary view that people died after drinking wine stored in yew barrels.

Teak

HIS TALL, elegant member of (surprisingly) the mint family has been known to grow as high as 40 metres (130 feet). Its small, dense clusters of fragrant, white flowers attract bees, their main pollinators, but the tree may also be wind-pollinated. With a straight, buttressed trunk, it has large, papery leaves – initially red but turning green as they mature. Teak trees produce a wood that is renowned for its great beauty and durability; its golden brown, lustrous hue darkens over time.

LATIN NAME *Tectona grandis*

HABITAT
Originally from Myanmar, Laos and Thailand in Asia, but now also found in India, Indonesia, Africa, the Caribbean, Costa Rica and South America.

Grows in both arid and moist tropical areas, monsoon forests and hillsides; from sea level to 915 metres (3,000 feet).

HISTORY
Teak has been used in boatbuilding for over 2,000 years.

In India and Myanmar, sturdy teak beams in palaces and temples may date back over a thousand years.

A teak tree in Thailand's Uttaradit Province is the world's oldest at some 1,500 years old.

Ancient kings of Burma and Thailand proclaimed teak to be a Royal Tree under strict royal protection.

MEANINGS
A symbol of eternity and strength.

SECRETS AND SPECIAL ASSOCIATIONS
Teak is a national symbol of Indonesia.

Teak's unique combination of natural oils means that it can withstand monsoon rains, sleet, snow and bacteria without rotting or developing mildew and fungi.

The oils also make it resistant to termite attacks.

India rubber trees seem to thrive in the presence of teak trees.

INTRIGUING INFORMATION
Teak's durable wood is water-resistant.

It is used for outdoor furniture, boats and boat decks, gangways, cutting boards, floors, carved items, countertops, doors, window frames, columns, beams, bridges and furnishing veneers.

Roots and leaves offer yellowish- and reddish-brown pigments used for dyeing paper and cloth.

The timber retains its aromatic fragrance to a great age.

Teak leaves are eaten in south India, Java and Indonesia, sometimes in jackfruit dumplings.

Care is taken that trees do not grow into the sky.
Johann Wolfgang von Goethe (1749–1832), Germany

What we are doing to the forests of the world is but a mirror reflection of what we are doing to ourselves and to one another.
Mahatma Gandhi (1869–1948), India

In fantastic over-scale, the trunks ... soar skywards under a shadowy
green canopy, their long spreading skirts trailing the ground and
their endless roots coiling more like reptiles than plants.
Maurice Glaize (1886–1964), France

Around a flowering tree, one finds many insects
Proverb from Guinea

Tetrameles

MEMBER OF the squash family, this large, deciduous tree has grey, shiny bark (sometimes yellow speckled) and small flowers with male and female blooms on separate trees. It grows 45 metres (148 feet) tall with a spreading, buttressed trunk containing large hollows. The columnar trunk can remain bare for up to 35 metres (115 feet). Fruits mature while the tree has only a few new leaves then dry into brown-yellow capsules that split open to release tiny seeds. The trees are famed for their enormous surface roots and especially for how these sprawl over ancient Cambodian temple ruins at Ta Prohm (part of the Angkor complex), creating a primeval landscape. Vast root systems snake over the porous, crumbling sandstone towers and walls, gripping them in a powerful, squid-like embrace and becoming part of the architecture.

LATIN NAME *Tetrameles nudiflora*

HABITAT

Central and eastern Asia and India, south to northern Australia.

It thrives in monsoon and rain forests in valleys, gallery forests on creek and river flats (especially at Cape York Peninsula, Australia), and limestone mountain slopes.

Tetrameles also needs a defined dry season.

HISTORY

Ta Prohm was built in the late 12th and early 13th centuries but mainly abandoned to nature when the Khmer Empire declined in the 15th century.

Scottish botanist Robert Brown provided the first European description of *Tetrameles nudiflora* in 1844 from material collected in Java.

MEANINGS

No official meaning but intimates tenacity, force, reciprocity.

SECRETS AND SPECIAL ASSOCIATIONS

Its hollow branches provide safe nesting sites for ruby-red and emerald eclectus parrots.

Until recently, dense, impenetrable jungle trees have kept most Khmer Empire cities and temples completely hidden.

INTRIGUING INFORMATION

Tetrameles is is too large for small gardens but is a popular ornamental tree in Asian parks.

It has poor quality wood so is mainly used only for temporary structures, boxes and matches.

However, in New Guinea canoes are made from tetrameles: rubbed with oil and hardened in salt water, these may last a decade.

Lime or Linden

LSO KNOWN in North America as basswood, this tree is different from the citrus lime, and first developed over 70 million years ago. It can live some 500 years, growing 40 metres (130 feet) tall with a sturdy, pillar-like trunk, a generous mantle of heart-shaped leaves and tiny, dangling, pea-like fruit. The blossom's intoxicating, heady scent summons bees; some overindulge and are overcome by a surfeit of nectar. Once recovered, they produce pale, rich honey. Lime hawk, peppered, vapourer, triangle and scarce hook-tip caterpillars chew the leaves while the sweet sap attracts hoverflies and ladybirds as well as aphids, which in turn are 'milked' by ants. Bees also sip the aphid honeydew. Ancient lime specimens may entice wood-boring beetles and birds seeking nest holes.

LATIN NAME *Tilia*

HABITAT
Temperate Northern Hemisphere: Europe, eastern North America and Asia.

HISTORY
Berlin's famous *Unter den Linden* boulevard was planted in 1647, replacing a bridle path leading to hunting grounds.
A 900-year-old lime tree at Nuremberg's Imperial Castle in Germany was planted by Holy Roman Empress Cunigundi.

MEANINGS
Conjugal love, romance, the 'tree of lovers'.
Also truth, fairness, justice and liberty.

SECRETS AND SPECIAL ASSOCIATIONS
Lime is the national tree of the Czech Republic, Slovakia and Slovenia.
Lime was a sacred tree in Slavic mythology.
It was a romantic symbol in medieval poetry.
Limes are said to protect against ill luck and lightning strikes.
Estonian and Lithuanian women made sacrifices to linden trees, requesting fertility and domestic bliss.
Germanic judicial cases were tried under a lime tree.

INTRIGUING INFORMATION
Lindens line many French avenues.
The wood is good for model-building, puppets, guitar bodies, recorders, drums, piano keys and icon panels.
Native Americans used fibres from soaked basswood bark (bast) for bags, baskets, belts, fishnets, mats, snowshoes, ropes and thread for sewing or suturing wounds.
The fibre also served to make Bronze Age and traditional Japanese clothing.
Germanic tribes made limewood shields.
Basswood seed and flower paste is a chocolate substitute.

If thou lookest on the lime-leaf,
Thou a heart's form will discover;
Therefore are the lindens ever
Chosen seats of each fond lover.
Heinrich Heine (1797–1856) Germany

Oh the scent of the limes on the linden tree!
Jeffrey Dolezal Hrbek (1882–1908), Czechoslovakia

*Let us take our hearts for a walk in the woods and listen
to the magic whispers of old trees.*
Unknown

*… the elms bent to one another, like giants who were
whispering secrets, and after a few seconds … fell into a
violent flurry, tossing their wild arms …*
Charles Dickens (1812–70), England

Elm

HE GENUS first appeared some 20 million years ago and today's species include American elm, English elm and wych elm as well as a large range in Asia. Some elms live for over 100 years and grow to a dizzy 30-40 metres (98–130 feet). The coarse, grey-brown, furrowed trunks often split so the tree fans out and in elm avenues this creates a nave of over-arching branches. Peppered, light emerald and white-spotted pinion moth caterpillars (plus those of white-letter hairstreak butterflies) gorge on the leaves. The seeds float down on papery wings and its seeds and fruits are relished (depending on geography) by bobwhite quail, prairie chickens, ruffed grouse and songbirds – as well as opossums and squirrels. America's sapsucker woodpeckers also love young elm trees.

LATIN NAME *Ulmus*
U. minor 'Atinia' (English elm)
U. glabra (wych elm)
U. Americana (American elm)

HABITAT
Originating in central Asia, elms spread throughout the Northern Hemisphere to North America and Eurasia.
It now ranges south into Indonesia.
Grows in natural forests, hedgerows, gardens, city streets, parks and coastal towns (elm tolerates salty sea spray).

HISTORY
Elms were grown as a shade tree in ancient Persia.
Some Minoan chariots and ancient Greek ploughs were made of elm.
In the Middle Ages it was used for bows – and longbows if yew was scarce.
The original piers of London Bridge were made from elm.
In both the French and American Revolutions, elms were planted as Liberty Trees.

Dutch elm disease (its fungal spores entering wounds caused by bark beetles) spread in the late 1960s; within a decade it had killed over 20 million trees in Europe and much of North America. Elms almost vanished from the landscape.

MEANINGS
Dignity.
Also melancholy and death; elm is often used for coffins.

SECRETS AND SPECIAL ASSOCIATIONS
In Germanic and Scandinavian mythology the first woman was formed from an elm.

INTRIGUING INFORMATION
Elm is used for Japanese drums, water pipes, ship keels and more.
It is a popular bonsai tree.

Small Trees and Shrubs

Bambusoideae Bamboos

Giant bamboos are the largest members of the grass family. All relish warm, moist, tropical and temperate climates, especially in the Asia-Pacific region. They include the world's fastest-growing plants that can stretch up 90 centimetres (36 inches) within a day. Its compressive and tensile strengths are greater than concrete and rival steel. Bamboo shoots are enjoyed in Asian dishes. Other creatures that eat bamboo include rats, chimpanzees, elephants, gorillas, golden bamboo lemurs and giant pandas.

Bamboo

Meanings: Chinese symbol of uprightness; Indian symbol of friendship. Linked to integrity, elegance and gentlemanly behaviour.

Bamboo is the national plant of St. Lucia.

Bamboo has served for houses, furniture, textiles, paper, weapons (bows, lances and martial-arts swords), bicycles, boats and rafts, skateboards, suspension bridges, fishing rods, flagpoles, flutes, drums and guitars.

Cercis siliquastrum Judas tree

From southern Europe and Western Asia, today it also flourishes in Malta, Pakistan and the USA – above the maquis scrub in more mountainous

Judas Tree
Meanings: Betrayal, disbelief.
In Israel the tree is protected.
The name Cercis comes from
    kerkis (Greek for a weaver's
    shuttle), to which the ancient
    botanist Theophrastus likened
    its woody fruits.
Flowers and young pods are
    edible and can be added to
    salads.
Leafcutter bees, caterpillars and
    beetles nibble the leaves.
Native Americans made a red
    dye from the roots.

regions. The spring overture of this beautiful, graceful tree is a prolific display of deep pink flowers that precede the heart-shaped leaves and glow on the trunk while their nectar summons bees from all around. The tree is perhaps named after the myth that Judas Iscariot hanged himself from it, so that its once pure white blossoms blushed red with shame while the wood turned brittle. Moreover, both the flowers and clusters of red-purple seedpods dangle like corpses. However, it is more likely that the name derives from the French common name Judea's tree (arbre de Judée). It is also known as the love tree or Eastern redbud.

Cornus Dogwood

Dogwood enjoys cooler areas of Europe, Western Asia and North America, especially forest edges, riversides and mountains. Creamy flower clusters are followed by black dogberries but the shrub is renowned for its purple, almost chocolate-coloured, autumn leaves and glorious winter stems – often fiery orange and red. Case-bearer moths nibble the leaves while both birds and mammals munch the berries. Native Americans used its root to attract muskrats into traps. Its straight stems have served as prods, butchers' skewers

Dogwood

Meanings: Durability and acceptance. A lady only accepted a dogwood blossom if she liked its sender – a returned flower meant unrequited love.

A prehistoric archer (nicknamed Otzi the Iceman), found frozen on the Italian/Austrian border in 1991, was carrying dogwood arrow shafts.

Some legends claim that because Jesus was crucified on a dogwood cross, God transformed this once tall tree into a small bush.

It has been used to treat malaria.

Cornus paniculata
Panicled Dogwood

(once called 'dogs'), cattle prods, toothbrushes, roller skates, tool handles, spindles, golf club heads and arrows.

Crataegus Hawthorn

Also known as thornapple, May-tree, whitethorn or hawberry, this is at home in temperate Northern Hemisphere zones of Europe, Asia and North America. These thorny shrubs and hedges offer food and shelter to wildlife including the small eggar moth, thrushes and waxwings, while nectar-feeding insects home in on the delicate flowers. Fruits of common hawthorn (which taste like over-ripe apples) are used in homemade wine and jellies while the

Hawthorn

Meanings: Hope.

Hawthorn is said to heal broken hearts.

Branches were carried in ancient Greek wedding processions.

Hawthorn is linked to Christ's crown of thorns; French peasants said it groaned on Good Friday.

When grown near holy wells in Celtic areas such as Ireland and Brittany in France, hawthorns are called rag trees, after the cloth strips tied to them during healing rituals.

edible young leaves and flower buds are sometimes called 'bread and cheese'.

Euonymus europaeus Spindle

Thriving on forest edges, hedges and gentle slopes in Europe (and today in North America), its deep green bark darkens with age and develops cork-like markings. Small, yellow-green flowers are succeeded by bright red, purple or pink fruits with orange seeds. These look like popcorn but eat them at your peril, for the poisonous fruits may induce liver and kidney damage, or even death. The leaves attract aphids (in turn nibbled by hoverflies, ladybirds and

Spindle

Meanings: Your charms are engraved upon my heart; for the Celts it meant sweetness and delight.

It was generally thought to be a lucky plant unless it flowered early, intimating imminent plague.

Its hard stems can be sharpened to a fine point and were used for making spinning spindles (giving it its common name), butchers' skewers, toothpicks, pegs and knitting needles.

It makes high-quality artists' charcoal.

lacewings) as well as house sparrows, plus spindle ermine, scorched carpet and magpie moth caterpillars – and those of the holly blue butterfly.

Ilex aquifolium Holly

Holly thrives worldwide from the tropics to temperate zones, from woodlands to mountainsides. The flowers provide nectar and pollen for bees while holly blue butterfly caterpillars and those of many moths eat the leaves. Its bright scarlet winter fruits, contrasting with the glossy, evergreen leaves, have long served as Christmas decorations. While the berries are toxic to humans (twenty or so may kill a child) these are an important food source for birds, wood mice and dormice but need to be first exposed to frost to soften up. Birds shelter from winter storms and predators in this prickly refuge while, down below, hedgehogs and small mammals hibernate in the dry leaf litter. The smoother leaves at the top are a winter treat for deer.

Holly

Meanings: Foresight; in heraldry it symbolizes truth; holly is also a fertility symbol.

It was thought to be unlucky to cut down a holly tree.

Romans sent holly boughs to friends during the Saturnalia winter festival.

In 'The Holly and the Ivy' carol, holly represents Jesus and ivy the Virgin Mary.

Its wood burns hotly and its charcoal was used to forge swords, knives and tools.

Druids associated holly with fire and wore it in their hair to ward off evil.

Laurus nobilis **Bay or Laurel**

Bay once flourished in humid laurel forests that covered much of the Mediterranean basin. Its glossy, aromatic leaves are much used in cooking to give a fragrant flavour to soups, stews and pasta, and it has many rich associations. In ancient Greece, a laurel wreath was the prize at the games held in Apollo's honour, while poets and scholars wore them when they received academic honours. The Romans crowned victorious military commanders

Bay or Laurel

Meanings: I change but in death; glory and reward of merit; prosperity, fame, victory.

The Greek god Apollo wore bay leaves after his beloved Daphne was changed into a bay tree by her father; *daphne* is the Greek name for this tree.

Poet laureate and baccalaureate derive from laurel's association with achievement.

'Resting on one's laurels' means relying on former glories.

The tree serves in topiary to create decorative ball- or box-shaped or twisted specimens, ideal for flanking an entrance.

with laurel leaves and today, bay circlets are still worn with pride by Italian students at graduation ceremonies.

Lavandula Lavender

Found across Europe, as well as in Africa, Asia and India, lavender is grown as an ornamental, a herb and for its gorgeous scent and essential oil. Elegant spikes of whorled flowers rise from green or silvery-grey foliage and bees love their abundant nectar. The Bible mentions it as a holy herb used in

Lavender

Meanings: Devotion; luck, success, happiness; distrust.

Lavender is used in teas and as a spice in pastas, stews, salads, dressings, sauces, bread, desserts, scones and marshmallows.

Lavender is perfect for dried flower arrangements.

Lavender sachets freshen linen and deter moths.

It is often added to potpourri and wedding confetti.

The extensive lavender fields in Provence, France, are a summer tourist attraction.

the Hebrew Temple. Lavender served in ancient Egyptian mummification and during the Black Death, bunches of lavender were sold in the streets to ward off both the plague and the smell of the corpses. In late medieval Europe it was used to perfume clothes or bed linen and to deter mice, flies and mosquitoes. Rather later, lavender essential oil was used in hospitals during World War I.

Myrtus Myrtle

These small, evergreen trees grow in Europe, Western Asia, India and North Africa; many are Mediterranean but some flourish in Saharan mountains. They have emerald, aromatic, leathery leaves, red or yellow berries and bowl-shaped, white flowers. Myrtles were a vital feature of Roman gardens. Mediterranean roasted pig is often stuffed with myrtle sprigs while the berries serve as a pepper substitute and are used in American bologna sausages.

Myrtle

Meanings: Love; a symbol of Eden; sacred in Venice.

Used by Jews in the Sukkot festival and also given to bridegrooms as a phallic, masculine symbol.

Myrtle was used in Roman wedding rituals.

It is used in Corsica and Sardinia to create Mirto, an aromatic liqueur.

A planted snip from Queen Victoria's wedding bouquet has ever since provided myrtle sprigs for British royal wedding bouquets.

Myrtle has been prescribed for fever and pain by physicians since at least 2500 BCE, and is used as a medicinal plant by Africa's Tuareg people.

It was beloved by Greek goddesses Aphrodite and Demeter. It is the tree of lovers because of this association with Aphrodite, the goddess of love.

Mountain Ash or Rowan

Meanings: Prudence;
delightful to the eye.

Rowan was once grown in
churchyards and beside
houses to protect them
from evil – the bright red of
the berries was regarded as
the best colour to ward off
witches.

Its pale, yellow-brown wood
was used for turning,
furniture, craftwork and
engraving, for stirring
milk to stop it curdling,
as a pocket charm against
rheumatism and to make
divining rods.

The berries are sour but rich in
vitamin C and make good
jellies.

Sorbus Mountain Ash or Rowan

Native to cooler Northern Hemisphere zones, hardy rowan often grows at high altitudes, especially in China and the Himalayas. The creamy white flowers offer pollen and nectar to bees and pollinating insects, while the scarlet fruits provide rich pickings for blackbirds, mistle thrushes, redstarts, redwings, song thrushes, fieldfares and waxwings, who disperse the seeds. Many moth caterpillars eat the leaves.

Syringa vulgaris Lilac

A member of the olive family, lilac is a native of rocky hills on the Baltic peninsula in Eastern Europe and Asia but is now grown in many parts of Europe. It was taken to North America by European colonists. Known as the Queen of Shrubs, there are more than 1,000 varieties all producing glorious and sweetly scented, cascading flowers in lavender, purple, pink or white.

Lilac

Meanings: Humility; first emotions of love; youthful innocence.

Lilacs are used in soaps, perfumes and other cosmetics.

Lilac wood can be used for turning and engraving or to make musical instruments, table legs, bowls, knife and pen handles.

Pan (the Greek god of nature) pursued a beautiful nymph named Syringa (lilac's Latin name) who escaped only by turning herself into a lilac.

Russian families used to hang a sprig over a baby to bring wisdom.

Viburnum opulus Guelder Rose

Native to Europe, northern Africa and Central Asia, the guelder rose enjoys damp lowlands along riversides, fens, scrub, thickets and old hedgerows or woods. Their leaves are similar to maple but have a wrinkled surface. Its white flowers arrive in early summer, to be pollinated by insects (hoverflies love them), while the berries are an important food source for bullfinches and mistle thrushes. It is also known as dogberry, water elder, cramp bark, snowball tree or European cranberry bush.

Guelder Rose

Meanings: Winter or age; its berries symbolize blood and the vitality of family roots.

A national symbol of Ukraine, featuring in many folk songs, art and embroidery.

The fruit can be used to make jelly but should be eaten cautiously as it is mildly toxic.

The bark can sooth muscle cramp and women's menstrual pains.

In Slavic paganism it represents the beauty of a young lady.

The Power of Trees

Trees as Treatments

From the moment herbal medicine began, extracts from trees have played their part, whether timber, bark, fruits, seeds, roots, leaves, sap or flowers. All around the world, from India to Ireland and from the Americas to Australia, human populations have learned to use the natural resources available to them in jungles, forests and small stands of trees. In the Western world, ancient historical tracts from Egypt, Greece and the Roman Empire, as well as medieval sources, described trees' amazing healing properties. From the 15th

Leaf tea.

century onwards, this Western knowledge was augmented by the revelation of multiple tree species from far-flung places, swept into view by new sea routes, greater contact with the Far East, and the discovery of the Americas and Australasia.

Today there is an increased drive to grasp the possibilities of and better understand alternative medicines, whether aromatherapy and the use of essential oils, or simply natural products that do not rely on artificial chemicals. The vast portfolio of ingredients drawn from trees is an important part of this process. Here are just a few ways that trees have been used as treatments:

Abies **Fir**: Resins and oils from the bark and foliage of true firs have a healing effect and are used in pharmaceuticals. Silver fir serves to treat joint pains, arthritis, muscle pains or cramps. Balsam fir is good for cuts, grazes and sores.

Acacia **Acacia or Wattle**: Ancient Egyptians ground the leaves to make a haemorrhoid ointment. Australian aboriginal people made a soothing wash for headaches, fever pains, and rheumatism (a treatment that was supposedly helped by resting under a possum-skin blanket). An infusion from the bark or roots soothed colds and laryngitis.

Acer **Maple**: A wash made from leaves can help wounds, and a poultice relieves sore eyes and breast discomfort in nursing mothers. Its bark tea treats kidney infections, the common cold and bronchitis.

Acer pseudoplatanus **Sycamore**: The sweet sap treats wounds, burns and skin ailments and helps with hair removal. Its bark has mild astringent properties and makes a skin tonic and an eyewash.

Adansonia digitata **Baobab**: Drinking a bark infusion is said to make men strong and serves as a malaria remedy. Baobab powder is a rich source of vitamin C with the highest antioxidant content of any fruit. In Africa, babies were bathed in baobab fruit infusions to soften their skin.

Baobab pod.

Almus **Alder**: Alder leaves placed in shoes before a journey cool the feet and prevent swelling. Invigorating alder tree oil reduces muscle stiffness and anxiety. The bark treats inflammations, rheumatism and diarrhoea. Bags filled with heated leaves ease sore skin and burns. A leaf and bark gargle soothes mouth ulcers and tonsillitis. Native American cultures used red alder bark to treat poison oak, insect bites and skin irritations. The Blackfeet people used bark infusions for lymphatic disorders and tuberculosis. Its astringent makes a good wash for wounds and a healing agent. Leaf and bark teas treat fever and (as a douche) haemorrhoids. Alder may help resist tumours.

Araucaria araucana **Monkey Puzzle**: A resin obtained from trunk incisions treats ulcers and wounds. Various components may help resist cancer, viruses, blood clotting and depression.

Arbutus **Madrone**: Arbutus bark and leaves help ease colds, sore throats, cramps, skin ailments, stomach ache and tuberculosis. It is a basis for contraceptives.

Betula **Birch**: Fragrant silver birch twigs are used in saunas to relax the muscles. Externally, silver birch helps healing, relieves pain and treats skin inflammations like eczema or psoriasis (by putting the bark in a bath). The leaves make diuretic teas that ease mouth sores, bladder and kidney problems, and gout. Birch may help reduce high blood pressure, cholesterol, obesity, kidney stones, cystitis, indigestion and respiratory problems. Soaked birch bark can make a cast for a broken arm. The sap might help reduce tumours and cancer.

Carpinus betulus **Hornbeam**: Hornbeam tonic is used to relieve both mental and physical exhaustion. The leaves staunch

Alder.

121

Eucalyptus

bleeding and improve wound healing. Bathing the eyes with hornbeam infusions helps treat infection and relieve puffiness. The inner bark acts as a purgative. Boiled bark can help relieve sore muscles, rheumatism and toothache. Massaging it into the scalp helps reduce hair loss.

Castanea dentata **American Chestnut**: Native Americans used it to treat heart conditions and inflamed skin. A gargled bark tea soothes inflamed tonsils; swallowed with honey it helps cure whooping cough.

Cedrus libani **Cedar of Lebanon**: Since the bark and the leaves are antiseptic and can act as an expectorant, the tea may be good for fevers, rheumatism, the flu and chest colds. Hebrew priests used cedar bark to treat leprosy.

Ceiba pentandra **Cotton Tree or Kapok**: The bark has been used to make aphrodisiacs and diuretics, and also to treat headaches and type 2 diabetes. Seeds, leaves, bark and resin may help dysentery, fever, asthma and kidney disease.

Cercis siliquastrum **Judas Tree**: The Alabama Native Americans used a cold root infusion for fevers and congestion. The Cherokee used it to treat coughs. Its roots have also been used as a purgative to induce vomiting.

Cornus **Dogwood**: This rich source of bitter-tasting tannins may soothe malaria. The bark tea also eases pain and fever. In Chinese medicine it treats dizziness, weakness, knee or back pain, uterine bleeding and sweating.

Crataegus **Hawthorn**: Leaf tea is a tonic for the heart and reduces blood pressure.

Diospyros **Ebony**: The roots treat dysentery, intestinal parasites, leprosy and fever. Ancient Egyptians used ebony wood shavings to soothe eye ailments.

Dracaena draco **Dragon Tree**: The resin may ease diarrhoea, superficial wounds, bleeding, ulcers, dysentery and fever.

Eucalyptus **Eucalyptus**: Aboriginal Australians use its oil as a potent disinfectant, antifungal and antibacterial agent. It soothes and treats asthma, bronchitis and chest colds. Its syrup honey is used internally and externally to treat respiratory troubles and arthritis. Inhaling the steam from boiling leaves clears blocked nasal passages. The crushed leaves make a wound antiseptic while pulverized bark reduces fatigue. Its aromatic oil is used in antiseptics, deodorizers, cough drops and toothpaste. Rainbow eucalyptus tea alleviates stress and purifies the blood.

Fagus sylvatica **Beech**: The leaves relieve swellings or may be boiled to make a poultice. Bark tea soothes lung problems and was once used for tuberculosis and to cleanse the blood. Leaf tea poultices ease frostbite and burns.

Ficus **Fig and Banyan**: The bark and leaves stop excessive wound bleeding. Figs were used in the Middle East to cure boils. Banyan latex may relieve pain and help cure piles, rheumatism and lumbago.

Fraxinus excelsior **Ash**: A twig and leaf tea may help reduce rheumatism, jaundice and gout. St. Hildegard of Bingen (1098–1179) recommended ash for gout and rheumatism. Some chemicals found in ash inhibit bacteria and fungi so it is good for healing wounds, sores and swelling. Ash bark might reduce fever, rickets and warts. The bark and leaves also lessen diarrhoea. It has been used against bladder and kidney ailments and to remove urinary tract stones.

Gleditsia triacanthos **Honey Locust**: Treats rheumatoid arthritis and cancer. Its tea can help indigestion, measles, whooping cough, catarrh and smallpox, while the pod juice is antiseptic.

Jacaranda mimosifolia **Jacaranda**: Essential oils and water extract are derived from the leaves, bark, fruits or flowers. In Brazil (where the jacaranda originated) it is recommended for treating bacterial infections, gonorrhoea and syphilis.

Juniperus **Juniper**: Good for the teeth and reducing diabetes. The berries speed up childbirth and may combat sciatica, asthma, bladder infections, upset stomachs, arthritis, bacteria and viruses. They also make a massage for sore joints and muscles, a wound antiseptic and an ointment to repel insects.

Larix **Larch**: All parts of the tree have medicinal properties but especially the flowers and berries. Its liquid, honey-coloured resin may be good for tuberculosis. Childless women once believed that spending the night under a larch would help them conceive a baby.

Laurus nobilis **Bay or Laurel**: Laurel leaves contain essential oils (including eucalyptol) that are antifungal and anti-itching and make an antibiotic cleanser as well as a soothing massage agent. Leaf or berry infusions are diuretic. It makes a salve for open wounds. *Dragon tree pods.*

Lavender oil.

Its compounds may inhibit breast and skin cancer cell production.

Lavandula **Lavender**: This is anti-inflammatory, antiseptic, a headache and indigestion remedy and a mosquito repellant. Lavender oil soothes aching muscles and joints, reduces anxiety and stress, and is a calming sedative that induces sleep.

Liquidambar styraciflua **Sweet Gum**: The antiviral and wound-healing sap helped Native Americans treat wounds, coughs, angina, sciatica and stomach problems. Its anti-inflammatory balm eases bedsores, ulcers and herpes. The fruit soothes rheumatic pain while the astringent bark is good for dysentery. The sweet, resinous sap was used in chewing gum and (during the two World Wars) to produce soaps, drugs, adhesives and ointments. Chewing twigs dipped in whisky may prevent diarrhoea. It is an active ingredient in flu injections.

Liriodendron tulipifera **Tulip Tree**: Its roots serve as a tonic and heart stimulant. Cherokee Native Americans used the inner bark and leaves for inflammation and sores. Its bark tea soothed fevers, diarrhoea, pinworms, toothache and rheumatic pain. The bark makes a quinine substitute if treating malaria and is a good cough syrup. The inner bark was once chewed as an aphrodisiac. Root, bark and seeds help expel parasitic worms.

Magnolia **Magnolia**: Bark and flower buds serve in traditional Chinese and Japanese medicine to improve lung health, relax muscles and treat anxiety. Magnolia is said to ease lung and chest congestion problems, menstrual cramps, indigestion and constipation. In Russia, herbalists sometimes prepare magnolia tree bark by soaking it in vodka.

Malus **Apple**: Its high boron levels improve memory and alertness and strengthen bones. It may protect against Parkinson's disease plus pancreatic, colon and breast cancers. It eases constipation, abdominal pain and bloating. Apple cider vinegar lowers type 2 diabetes blood sugar levels, makes hair

Dates.

shine and, added to bathwater, soothes sunburn. Its bark treats fevers and diarrhoea. Stewed apples make a laxative while baked apples soothe fevers and sore throats.

Morus **Mulberry**: Improves the blood, eases stress, constipation, diabetes, gout, tooth decay, haemorrhage, ringworm and snakebites. Bark is good for coughs, wheezing, fever, food poisoning, headache and sore eyes. The Romans used the leaves to treat mouth, trachea and lung diseases.

Myrtus **Myrtle**: This was prescribed for fever and pain by physicians back in 2,500 BCE. Its high levels of salicyclic acid help clear sinus infections, reduce respiratory issues, protect intestines, prevent some cancers, treat skin problems, control blood sugar levels, improve kidney function and boost heart health.

Olea europaea **Olive**: Olives help quench thirst, have natural antihistamines, and treat sore throats, laryngitis, whooping cough and dysentery. They can help reduce coronary artery and nerve diseases, bone loss, osteoporosis and cancer risk. The leaves stabilize blood sugar, controlling diabetes. Ancient Egyptians used olives in mummification. In the 1800s, a crushed olive leaf beverage was used to lower fevers and olive tea was a malaria treatment.

Pine.

Phoenix dactylifera **Date Palm**: Decreases cholesterol, treats constipation, and boosts energy levels and bone health. The juice soothes coughs and breathing problems.

Picea **Spruce**: Resin and oils extracted from the bark of spruce are ingredients of various ointments used for rheumatism, muscle ache and poor blood circulation. Native Americans used the resin that leaks from an injured spruce tree to ease thirst.

Pinus **Pine**: Good for chest coughs and massaging sore muscles. Warm pine sap will ease skin infections and pain. The pollen is a tonic, rich in vitamins and minerals. Peeled twigs can be chewed to prevent bad breath.

Platanas **Plane**: The astringent inner bark serves as an emetic and laxative;

Cherry.

it has been used as a tonic tea to treat dysentery, coughs, colds, lung ailments, haemorrhages, measles and urine infections, and to wash wounds, infected sores or baby rash. Root and bark infusions make good foot soaks and soothe rheumatism. The bark mixed with that of honey locust makes a gargle for hoarse or sore throats.

Populus **Poplar**: The Greeks used this to treat gout. Native Americans and European settlers in America discovered that aspen bark contains a quinine substitute. Various parts served to treat dysentery, arthritis, burns, inflammation, warts, wounds, ulcers and haemorrhoids.

Prunus **Cherry and Plum**: Cherries can help to prevent memory loss. They serve as a diuretic and ease kidney pain, swollen eyes and acne. They can be used instead of digitalis to make the heartbeat stronger. Boiled dried plums may deter diabetes. Plums can also reduce cholesterol, relieve constipation, improve cardiovascular health and boost the immune system.

Pyrus **Pear**: With excellent dietary fibre, pears are good for the skin. They offer nutrients, antioxidants, anti-inflammatory flavonoids and anticancer phytonutrients, while helping weight loss and hypertension.

Quercus **Oak**: Oak bark helps to treat rectal bleeding, uterine bleeding and gastrointestinal tract inflammation. Compresses soaked in bark decoctions may soothe varicose veins, eye inflammations, rashes, itching and eczema, while gargles can help ease sore throats and tonsillitis. Ointments treat haemorrhoids and minor burns. Powdered bark acts upon both nasal polyps and eczema. Oak galls may serve in place of the bark if used in smaller quantities. Acorns also serve in skin care, can improve digestion, keep bones healthy and help resistance to diabetes.

Salix **Willow**: Ancient healers made leaf and bark preparations as remedies for fever, pain and rheumatism. Native Americans used to eat weeping willow bark to cure headaches while its flower teas cured toothache. Today salicylic acid is extracted from the tree and used to make aspirin. Willow is anti-inflammatory and might help treat bleeding, heartburn and stomach ailments.

Willow bark.

Sequoiadendron giganteum **Redwood**: Can counter the build-up of mucus, especially in the lungs, and is good for rheumatism.

Swietenia **Mahogany**: This is good for the skin and counteracts erectile dysfunction. The bark treats diarrhoea, offers vitamins and iron, clears the blood, increases appetite, and restores strength. Tea from bark or seeds may also reduce fever and stop toothache and chest pains. The fruit makes an energy drink that helps blood circulation and might contribute to lowering cholesterol.

Taxus baccata **Yew**: A chemical found in yew, called taxol, has anticancer effects; it has now been synthesized and is used to treat breast, ovarian and lung cancers. Otherwise, all parts of the tree are poisonous and can impact on nerves, heart, and muscles; eating just a few leaves can make a small child critically ill. Nonetheless, yew has served to treat diphtheria, epilepsy, tonsillitis and tapeworms.

Tectona grandis **Teak**: Various parts are used to treat bacterial and fungal infections, ulcers, constipation, dysentery, urinary tract disorders, bronchitis, nausea and diabetes. It may prevent asthma attacks, destroy parasitic worms and reduce skin inflammation.

Tilia **Lime or Linden**: The flowers, leaves, wood and charcoal are used. Taken internally, linden flowers can help soothe nervous conditions, epilepsy, hypertension, insomnia, migraines, feverish colds, coughs and sore throats. They are antiseptic and anti-inflammatory. Used externally, the flowers soothe cracked or irritated skin and insect bites. The wood may ease liver and gallbladder disorders and cellulitis.

Ulmus **Elm**: Native Americans used various elm parts to treat broken bones, gunshot wounds, diarrhoea and coughs. The inner bark creates a soothing, protective film; bark salve and poultices soothe chilblains and help draw out fever. Its high-calcium bark tea may help injured bones to mend, heal sore throats and ease urinary or bowel issues. It once served to treat ringworm.

Lime or linden.

Trees as Inspiration

Trees through the seasons

Spring

Whereas tropical regions experience just two seasons (dry and rainy), in temperate zones spring is one of four seasons, and is the time when many plants begin to grow and flower. In the Northern Hemisphere this generally takes place from late February and March through to May while the Southern Hemisphere is experiencing its autumn (fall). At the spring equinox the days are about twelve hours long with day length increasing as the season progresses. Once the days become a little longer and warmer, tree roots spring into action, transferring water and nutrients from the soil into the rest of the tree. Hidden behind the bark, as the water begins to move, it mixes with simple sugars to create sap. Then, as this sap rises up the tree, fresh leaves unfurl and the trees grow taller. In this way the tree uses chlorophyll, carbon dioxide, water and sunlight to create carbohydrates that act as its food. Soon the over-wintered buds open and flowers emerge. Many trees, such as magnolias, cherries, almonds and quince, produce glorious blossom. The trees spread pollen, using wind or animals or floating seeds. This is the season of rebirth and hope.

As such it is greatly celebrated in the USA, with major cherry blossom festivals in Washington, plus celebrations in Philadelphia, San Francisco, Georgia, Newark, Salem, St. Louis and Nashville. Other places around the world that welcome spring blossom in style include the French cities Nice, with its carnivals, and Saint-Tropez, with its mimosa festival. But it is Japan that wears the blossom crown with its famous *Hanami* ('flower-viewing'), the traditional custom of marking the transient beauty of blossom, especially that of the cherry, plum and wisteria. It was the Japanese Emperor Saga (786–842) of the Heian period who first adopted this practice, and held flower-viewing parties with sake and feasts underneath the blossoming boughs

Plum, cherry and sloe blossom.

of *sakura* (cherry) trees in Kyoto's imperial court. Poems honoured the delicate flowers, which were seen as a metaphor for ephemeral life, luminous and inspiring yet over all too quickly. Today in Japan there are still picnics and feasts, sake drinking and night festivities lit by colourful paper lanterns to celebrate the *sakura* season.

Summer

Forests cover one third of the earth's surface in tropical, temperate and boreal zones – experiencing dry, wet, humid, freezing cold and fiercely hot climates. Seasonal changes depend on whether the trees are evergreen or deciduous, and also on geography. For example, in South Asia's monsoon areas, summer runs from the warmest days of early June and finishes in late September. Generally, midsummer is celebrated at the summer solstice when the days reach their longest. At this time trees are in full leaf and at the peak of their rich splendour. Most of the buds (containing next year's leaves) are set by midsummer. Growth then slows and the enzymes that power photosynthesis cease to function during the hottest hours. The canopy casts more shade over the woodland floor but, in sunnier glades in some countries, butterflies still

Sunlight shines into a forest in summer.

flit over forest plants such as red campion, orchids and honeysuckle. No longer raising young, birds sing less and less. In areas of drought, fire may be a threat but is sometimes part of the ecological pattern, triggering a rush of new growth and germination.

Autumn (Fall)

As children collect the last of the blackberries, hazelnuts and chestnuts, creatures such as squirrels, wood mice and jays also gather their winter stores and wild boar snuffle out acorns. The days grow colder and shorter, while leaves create less chlorophyll and so take on their glorious autumn golds and russet reds before tumbling from the trees. Suddenly there is scant cover for animals to hide from predators. Autumn crocus, cyclamen and honeysuckle continue to bloom in the forest while ivy, which flowers late in the year, provides a valuable source of nectar for some insects before they hibernate. Birds collect in flocks, many set to migrate. Deer stags and bucks develop antlers and fight rival males. Meanwhile, although fungi grow all year round, generally autumn is the best time to discover an impressive array of mushrooms and toadstools in the forest. Cobwebs glint with raindrops or dew as mist swirls over the woodlands, the low angle of the sun slanting through in shafts – followed by spectacular sunsets, large moons and night stars that seem extra bright above the tree tops.

Winter

Hormones flood through the tree cells to prevent winter dehydration as they are also infused with compounds that help prevent their freezing. Frost highlights the intricate pattern of bare branches or swathes of evergreen needles. Night owls continue to swoop on unwary prey but now many creatures – hedgehogs, dormice, bears and bats – are hibernating. Foraging voles, shrews, mice, hares, foxes, badgers and deer, however, still leave their tracks on fresh snow. This is the perfect

A Christmas tree is a common symbol of midwinter in the Northern Hemisphere.

time to appreciate the silhouettes of delicate silver birch or muscular oaks, forests with countless crisscrossed limbs hatching across pale skies, ash twigs like witches' claws, and willows weeping their own blizzard of snowflakes. Sometimes the wind sends bare branches clacking together but often, especially when shrouded in snow, the forest is quiet and still. It is resting now, restoring its energies – holding its breath until spring.

Art and artists

Painters and illustrators have ever been inspired by the natural landscape, with trees a major source of artistic stimulation. In ancient times Egyptian pharaohs nurtured trees and valued their timber, importing ebony from the Sudan, plus pine and cedar from Syria. They planted acacia, willow and sycamore figs, and many are depicted in their tombs. Trees have ever since been an important element in the visual arts. Here are just a few examples to remind us how dynamic a subject they can prove to be – and how very differently each can be portrayed.

Ancient Egypt: Many tree products were used in the embalming and mummification of bodies or for coffins. These included juniper oil, cedar wood and resins from several trees. A relief recording Hatshepsut's expedition to the Land of Punt shows Egyptian soldiers bearing tree branches. A trading partner

Reliefs recording Hatshepsut's expedition to the Land of Punt show Egyptian soldiers bearing either whole trees or tree branches.

of Egypt, the ancient kingdom of Punt (possibly in Somalia) was known for the export of aromatic resins and ebony.

Albert Bierstadt (1830–1902): A German-American painter, he was inspired by the American West and depicted the rugged beauty of the great outdoors, including landscapes with trees.

Paul Cézanne (1839–1906): Cézanne was a French artist with many works motivated by trees. His fresh thinking aroused great interest and spearheaded the twentieth-century's more radical approach to art.

Poplars on the Epte *by Claude Monet.*

Gustav Klimt (1862–1918): An Austrian symbolist painter, with his brother, Ernst (an engraver like their father) and a friend, Franz Matsch, he formed the 'Company of Artists'. While Klimt's work mainly depicted women and was often erotic, trees were also part of his repertoire.

Piet Mondrian (1872–1944): This renowned Dutch artist was a pioneer of abstract art. His earlier paintings, in particular, include depictions of trees in various landscapes and moods including a red tree, willows, oak trees and apples in bloom.

Claude Monet (1840–1926): Monet was one of the founders of the French Impressionist painting movement. As a young boy, he sold charcoal caricatures to locals but in due course studied how to paint using outdoor techniques. Among Monet's most famous subjects are weeping willows and poplar trees.

Camille Pissarro (1830–1903): Pissarro was a Danish-French Impressionist and Neo-Impressionist painter born in what was then the Danish West Indies (now the US Virgin Islands). He helped establish and maintain a collective society of fifteen aspiring artists, and nearly all of his paintings featured trees.

Henri Rousseau (1844–1910): A French Post-Impressionist 'primitive' painter, he is best known for his depiction of jungle scenes. Self-taught with 'no teacher other than nature', his exotic landscapes positively glow.

Vincent van Gogh (1853–1890): Post-Impressionist Dutch painter van Gogh painted in relative obscurity until after his death, since when his genius has evoked widespread, unabated popularity. Many of his works depict trees.

Trees in stories and music

Individual trees of many kinds and forests en masse appear in just about all artistic media including literature, theatre, ballet and music in all its forms. In fantasy novels and children's stories, forests often represent the 'unknown' and may be full of danger, such as J.R.R. Tolkien's Mirkwood in *The Hobbit* and his Forest of Fangorn in *The Lord of the Rings*. There were snow-filled, everlasting-winter forests in *The Lion, The Witch and the Wardrobe* by C.S. Lewis, while the Forbidden Forest and the Whomping Willow provide stimulating tree surroundings in the Harry Potter series by J.K. Rowling. Nearly two-thirds of the tales penned by the Brothers Grimm take place in forests. Rudyard Kipling's *The Jungle Book* offers a more exotic, Indian jungle setting. *Where the Wild Things Are* by Maurice Sendak features a forest that grows tall in Max's room as trees thrust up from the floor – at first this is a dark and threatening place but it soon translates into a scene of dancing and frolic. In A. A. Milne's *Winnie the Pooh,* the Hundred-Acre Wood is a gentle place with deciduous trees including large oaks and beech trees. Even city parks can offer interesting trees, such as those in J.M. Barrie's *Peter Pan in Kensington Gardens*. Meanwhile, *A Walk in the Woods* by Bill Bryson discovers breathtaking woodland terrain along America's Appalachian Trail.

Individual trees may assume symbolic roles, such as the oak tree that represents friendship in Harper Lee's *To Kill a Mockingbird* or the tree that demonstrates perseverance and hope amidst hardship in *A Tree Grows In Brooklyn* by Betty

Smith. Baobab trees grow ferociously and need to be guarded against in *The Little Prince* by Antoine de Saint-Exupéry. By contrast, Enid Blyton's *The Magic Faraway Tree* offers pure escapism and wish-fulfilling fun.

In the worlds of theatre and performance, William Shakespeare's Desdemona sings about a willow tree in *Othello* while poor wretched Ophelia drowns by one in *Hamlet*; in *A Midsummer Night's Dream,* the trees supply magic, fairies and escapism. Pyotr Ilyich Tchaikovsky's ballets

In the fairy tale Hansel and Gretel, *the children wander, lost in the forest.*

Forests easily take on an air of enchantment.

include woodland settings in *The Nutcracker Suite, The Sleeping Beauty* and *Swan Lake*, while in the opera *Daphne* by Richard Strauss, the heroine assumes a tree form. The play *Dear Brutus* by J.M. Barrie introduces a mystical woodland setting, while *Xerxes* by George Frideric Handel includes an ode to a plane tree. In Richard Wagner's *Die Walküre,* Sieglinde lives in a forest hut with an ash tree growing inside! Tree settings feature in *Tales from the Vienna Woods*, the play by Ödön von Horváth set to music by Johann Strauss the Younger. Meanwhile, in Giacomo Puccini's *Madame Butterfly*, Cio-Cio-San and Suzuki trill a duet about cherry tree blossom, while Mathilde sings of the forest in Gioachino Rossini's *William Tell.*

Nor do films escape the emotive forest influence. Consider *Bambi, Into the Woods* and *Snow White* ... Or for an adult audience, *The Blair Witch Project, Cabin Fever, Deliverance* and the *Planet of the Apes* series, not to mention the *Tarzan* movies, of course.

Wherever one turns, trees offer inspiration and beauty, providing spectacular settings for every possible medium.

Spirit of the Forest

A forest can be a sanctuary, a place of peace, and even a single tree in a garden offers solace and comfort. A baby in its pram will watch the dancing leaves and seem content. A child climbs up into the branches and discovers somewhere to escape to and dream, looking down on the world below from a new perspective.

Today we talk of 'hugging trees', and there is scientific evidence that getting close to trees is good for us: it can ease depression, lower blood pressure, slow the heart rate, help concentration levels and alleviate headaches. Although the 'hugging' term is modern, this practice has been going on since ancient times. The Japanese have long advocated 'forest bathing' – simply spending time in a forest – as a means of reducing stress, boosting the immune system and improving overall feelings of well-being.

Special trees were often the focal point for village meetings, community events and weddings. Bedouin Arabs certainly appreciated the shade of a tree as a cool meeting place. In central Europe, the most venerable oak became the 'justice tree' where the magistrate sat to pass judgment; many a villain has been hanged from a tree.

In many parts of the world it also became the custom to tie wreaths or ribbons to sacred trees, perhaps seeking the mediation of a saint or simply making a wish. In some areas, people left money under the tree as an offering to the supernatural world, hoping to ensure the fulfillment of some important need or desire. So trees

A tree linked to a Hindu temple in India.

In the fairy tale of Little Red Riding Hood, *the woods offer both comfort (her grandmother's house) and danger (the wolf).*

– and the places between them – became temples of one sort or another. Today, no Buddhist or Hindu shrine is complete without a sacred tree planted nearby. Trees and forests encourage our spiritual life.

All around the globe, the forest interacts with the elements and may be a place of calm, glades dimpled with woodland flowers. However, when darkness falls … or the wind rushes through the leaves … and branches creak … or lightning strikes … or a forest fire wreaks havoc, the forest can mutate into a place of terror.

Perhaps this is why woods have been the backdrop to so many folk tales, legends and mysteries. From medieval times onwards fairies, witches, sorcerers, gnomes, trolls, centaurs and unicorns were said to be discovered in their depths, and collectors of folktales such as the Russian Alexander Nikolayevich Afanasyev, the German Brothers Grimm and Frenchman Charles Perrault gathered together many fairy tales in which heroes and heroines were guided into forests – vast, dark places where dangerous, wild creatures lurked. Here Snow White ran from the wicked queen, the wolf tricked Red Riding Hood, and Hansel and Gretel very nearly met sorry ends in the Gingerbread House.

An Indian holy man who has chosen a very common setting, the shade of a tree, to sit in a yoga position and meditate.

The ancient Greeks and Romans thought that trees were inhabited by nymphs such as dryads. Druids met in forest glades, where their most sacred plant, mistletoe, looped in cloudy drifts through the branches. In medieval Europe, witches were said to make their brooms from willow tree branches and in Merrie England, Robin Hood gathered his band of outlaws in Sherwood Forest.

With so many myths and tree lore, the forest becomes a force not only of nature but also of our own internal spirit, our self-knowledge and growth. This is an elemental place, somewhere to commune with the primordial world and stir every sense: we feel pine needles, soft grass or mossy paths beneath our feet; we hear birdsong and rustling leaves or the wind in branches above; we touch the rough bark and shiny, sharp holly; we relish the forest fruits; we rejoice in the tang of wet rain on earth and the forest scents. We see so much awe-inspiring beauty all around that the forest becomes a place not only to discover nature, but also to discover so much more about ourselves.

Tree mysticism

Abies **Fir**: Tall firs suggest a clear vision of what is beyond and yet to come. Fir is also the birth tree; their needles were burned to protect a new mother and baby.

Acer **Maple**: Native Americans regarded this as the tree of offering – full of imagination, originality and energy.

Adansonia digitata **Baobab**: African Bushmen believed there were spirits inside the flowers; if you plucked these you might be savaged by lions. However, soaked baobab pips protected you from crocodiles.

Almus **Alder**: This was thought to be protected by water sprites and offered a charm against malevolent fairies.

Arbutus **Madrone**: This sacred tree is never used for firewood by the Canadian Salish people because it provided an anchor for canoes during the Great Flood.

Betula **Birch**: Associated with healing magic, truth and new beginnings, this was said to bestow fertility on newlyweds. Babies' cradles were made from it, and criminals were birched to drive out evil influences.

Corylus avallana **Hazel**: This is used for magic wands, seeking buried treasure and discovering knowledge.

Crataegus **Hawthorn**: Witches and fairy folk are said to revere hawthorn. Its wood provides powerful magical wands.

Fagus sylvatica **Beech**: Beech is concerned with ancient knowledge and inspires creativity, leadership and companionship. It symbolizes tolerance.

Fraxinus excelsior **Ash**: It features in Egyptian, Assyrian, Indian, Persian, Scandinavian and Native American mythology. Ash was the Nordic 'World Tree', and Vikings believed the first man was created from ash. Its leaves under your pillow are held to stimulate psychic dreams. Placing its berries in a cradle was thought to protect the child from becoming a changeling.

Ilex **Holly**: Holly is associated with winter, death and rebirth in both pagan and Christian lore. It is thought to enhance magical protection, prophecies and healing. A bag of leaves and berries is said to increase a woman's attraction to a man.

Juglans **Walnut**: Native Americans believe the tree conveys mental wisdom and helps with astral travel.

Larix **Larch**: This is said to protect against enchantment and to induce visions. It plays an important role in Sami and

Simply walking through a forest can make us feel more content.

Apples offer beauty and happiness.

Siberian mythology; their shamans use its wood for ceremonial drum rims.

Malus **Apple**: Apples offer beauty and happiness. In Norse myths, Apples of Immortality kept the gods young. The Isle of Avalon, where Celtic heroes like King Arthur rest, means 'Apple Island'.

Olea **Olive**: This symbolizes good fortune as well as peace. In ancient Greece an Athenian bride would wear an olive crown to ensure her fertility, while single people used the leaves to attract a spouse.

Picea **Spruce**: In Native American culture the spruce has great healing knowledge.

Pinus **Pine**: The 'sweetest of woods' and Native American 'tree of peace', pine helps alleviate guilt and purify the home. Its cones and seeds serve as fertility charms while a bag of needles in a bath provides magical cleansing and stimulation.

Populus **Poplar and Aspen**: They are linked to the winds, inciting fear and anxiety but dispelling anger, doubt or terror. It was said that Christ's cross was made of aspen so its leaves quiver in remembrance.

Prunus **Cherry**: The fruit is linked to the life forces of sex and birth.

Pyrus **Pear**: Ancient Germanic tribes carved runes into the wood of fruit trees, most likely the pear.

Quercus **Oak**: The druids associated oak with protection, success, fertility, health and good luck. Oak galls, known as serpent eggs, were used in magical charms. Rustling oak leaves and wrens hiding within were thought to pass on divinatory messages.

Salix **Willow**: This is associated with moon magic. Celtic priests and priestesses sat in willow groves to gain inspiration or to prophesy, while ordinary folk made wishes by tying loose knots in bendy willow shoots.

Sequoiadendron giganteum **Redwood**: These draw down power from heaven and help create spells of mystical union with nature and wild creatures.

Sorbus **Mountain Ash or Rowan**: This tree protects against enchantment and assists healing and psychic powers. Rowan sticks were used for carving runes and for wands, amulets and spells.

Taxus baccata **Yew**: Yew enhanced magical and psychic abilities and visions. It has been associated with death, reincarnation and immortality. It was linked to the Norse runes.

Tilia **Lime or Linden**: Pagan gods were thought to inhabit limes but were replaced by the Virgin Mary, whose image was often glimpsed in its dark branches. Lime was used for icon painting and church carvings. It was thought that lightning would not hit this tree, so people sheltered beneath it during thunderstorms.

Ulmus **Elm**: In Celtic and Greek myths elm trees were associated with tombs and the underworld. The Japanese Ainu goddess, Kamuy Fuchi, was born from an elm. Elms also stabilize spells.

A forest is a place to think about nature and oneself.

Fungi and other parasites

For centuries, fungi were thought to indicate the presence of evil spirits, elves or witches. Today we know better, but there are still mysteries to be uncovered as so much of the world of fungi takes place out of sight and underground. Toadstools and mushrooms are fleeting fruiting bodies, but they tell us that down below are spread long-lived, underground fungal threads, called hyphae. The hyphae link to form a mass called a mycelium, and some can live for hundreds or even thousands of years. The toadstool fairy rings – seen in so many illustrations of fairy tales – are made up of fruiting bodies emerging around the edge of a mycelial disc.

Those who accept (as many do) that trees and plants communicate, believe that fungi have a good deal to do with this. Their vast, undercover network of fine mycelia threads creates a veritable information superhighway that speeds up contact between plants by linking their roots. Sharing both nutrients and 'news' it offers, moreover, the opportunity, when needed, to spread toxic chemicals through the system to ward off enemies. Fungal networks also boost their hosts' immune systems, triggering the production of defence chemicals that make them more resistant to disease. As a result of her research, Suzanne Simard of the University of British Columbia in Vancouver believes that large trees help out smaller, younger ones using these fungal links.

Fungi have been called 'Earth's natural Internet' and few places have as many fungi as woodland areas. Countless mushrooms and toadstools flourish amid autumnal forests, some offering a welcome feast to scavengers. Moreover, without them the forest floor would be buried under layers of needles, leaves, dead animals and fallen branches – fungi called saprophytes feed on and break down dead matter and thus return the nutrients to the soil. Certain fungi are able to use enzymes to biodegrade lignin (a polymer in cell walls that makes wood tough and rigid), and have an especially crucial role to play in maintaining the life cycle of a forest.

In places like France where there are many chestnut, pine and oak forests, wild mushrooms like the cep (*Boletus edulis*) flourish, as do delicious black Périgord truffles, while in northern Italy, Alba white truffles tempt the taste buds and are still today snuffled out by pigs and dogs. Many fungi serve as food for birds,

Amanita pantherina
Panthercap mushroom

Russula emetica
Emetic russula

Phallus impudicus
Stinkhorn

Lactarius torminosus
Wooly milkcap

Amanita muscaria
Fly agaric

Suillellus luridus
Lurid bolete

Amanita phalloides
Death cap mushroom

Rubroboletus satanas
Devil's bolete

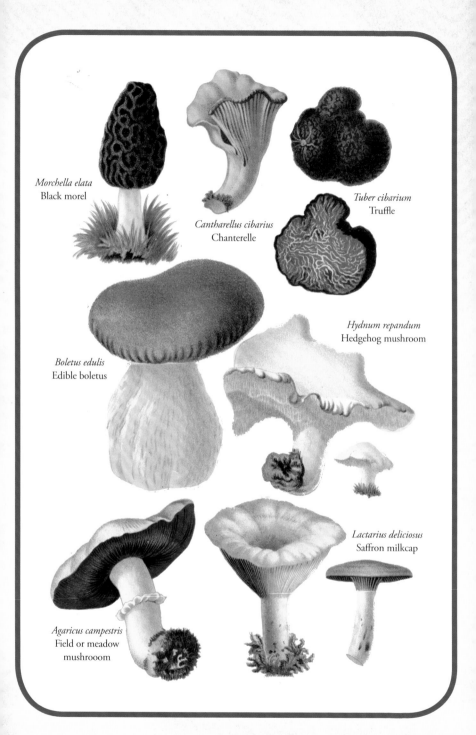

Morchella elata
Black morel

Cantharellus cibarius
Chanterelle

Tuber cibarium
Truffle

Boletus edulis
Edible boletus

Hydnum repandum
Hedgehog mushroom

Agaricus campestris
Field or meadow
mushrooom

Lactarius deliciosus
Saffron milkcap

mammals, amphibians and reptiles. Slugs munch away at them, too, while rodents such as voles and squirrels store them somewhere safe for winter feasts. However, fungi are not always so delicious or benign. Some toadstools, in particular, can be toxic and hallucinogenic. The red, spotted toadstools so often seen supporting mischievous elves in children's tales are poisonous hallucinogens called fly agaric (*Amanita muscaria*). A good number of fungi, some with quite dramatic architectural structures, are parasites and will weaken – or even ultimately kill – their host trees. Initially many grow discreetly but, as time progresses, they deplete the tree's resources and energy. These include the honey fungus or honey mushroom (*Armillaria mellea*). The bracket fungus *Phellinus tremulae* is also parasitic, although its nooks and crannies do provide a haven for insects such as beetles and moths.

Of course, this cycle of life ensures the woodland certain benefits: dead and decaying trees provide great habitats for beetles, flies, spiders and bats, as well as birds such as woodpeckers, ospreys, crested tits and owls, which all nest in them. Moreover, woodland glades and young trees benefit greatly by the increased light levels, thus enriching diversity.

Meanwhile some insects 'collaborate' with fungus to attack trees. For example, the fungal genus *Septobasidium* has developed a parasitic relationship with scale insects that feed on tree bark. This insect sinks its proboscis into the bark of a tree and remains there for the rest of its life, sucking sap. The mycelium of *Septobasidium* then creates elaborate structures over colonies of the scale insects, feeding from the parasitized insects but leaving them alive. Another example of insects working with fungi is found in the tropical forests of Central and South America, where busy leafcutter ants cultivate fungi in their nests as an ongoing food supply.

INTRIGUING INFORMATION

Some fungi will grow only with one kind of tree; for example, the bolete *Gyrodon lividus* grows only under alders.

When the top of a ripe puffball explodes like a volcano, it shoots out *millions* of tiny spores.

Bracket fungi can support entire mini-ecosystems.

The world's largest living organism is a honey fungus that covers more than 809 hectares or 8 square kilometres (2,000 acres) and may be some 2,400 years old. It lives mostly underground in the Blue Mountains of Oregon, USA.

Earth may host more than 5 million fungi species.

Forests in Crisis

While in some European countries such as France and Germany forests are once again increasing, sadly this is certainly not the case worldwide. As the preceding chapters have shown, our woodlands provide a vast range of important products – from essential fuel to wood for buildings, furniture, ships and canoes, as well as materials for dyes, baskets, fishing nets, tannin and much more. All the various tree parts (bark, roots, leaves, flowers, sap, resin, fruits or seeds) offer both nourishment and medicinal products – as do the mushrooms that thrive in the shadow of trees. Forests are home to well over half the globe's land-based animal and plant species. Within forests so many species depend one upon another, in ways that we do not yet thoroughly appreciate, that we upset the balance at our peril.

Moreover, these are places that restore our spiritual well-being. We feel re-energized by being among trees. We seem to commune with them, to feel some sense of empathy, to understand ourselves better and thus, with trees in our lives, we are able look ahead to a happier future.

The world has already lost half its natural forests.

Less than 10 per cent of the planet's land area remains as unspoiled forest landscape.

82 nations within the original forest zone of 148 countries have lost every single intact forest.

In areas of greatest forest loss or degradation, up to 1.7 million square kilometres (656,373 square miles) of forest may well be destroyed by 2030 – equivalent to an area stretching across Germany, France, Spain and Portugal.

1.5 hectares (15,000 square metres or 3.7 acres) of rainforest disappear due to deforestation every second.

However, that future may not be all we imagine and hope for if the needs of the trees and those species that depend upon them are not taken into account.

Trees have vital environmental roles to play, both locally and on a global scale, but this has largely been ignored in the rush to fell trees (often illegally) to find fuel, to build with timber, to mine minerals, to build roads or railways and dams while seeking ever more space for homes and farming to grow cash crops like soya or palm oil.

As well as the Amazon rainforest, we have plundered the other tropical forests of Latin America, Africa, Indonesia and much of the Asia Pacific regions, plus the great boreal forests of Russia, Canada and Alaska. This deforestation can impact upon rainfall, weather and rising sea levels *everywhere* from the American Midwest, to Europe and China.

Over half of the approximate 10 million species of plants, animals and insects on the globe live in tropical rainforests.

We lose 137 species (plant, animal and insect) every day – 50,000 species a year – as rainforests are felled or burned.

Soil Erosion

On a local scale, tree roots stabilize soil to prevent flooding and erosion, while a forest canopy shields the ground from the effects of weather. After deforestation, the exposed, thin soil soon degrades and blows away, unable to resist wind and rain erosion without the protection of the trees' binding roots and their overhead cover.

Carbon Sinks

As well as stabilizing a local environment, trees serve a vital role for the Earth. Our worldwide weather patterns depend upon an intricate global

The incredible diversity of life in the Amazon rainforest.

> More than 20 per cent of the world's oxygen is produced in the Amazon rainforest.
> Tropical deforestation is the world's second greatest contributor to climate change, after greenhouse gas emission.
> The Amazon Basin holds one-fifth of the world's fresh water.
> Moisture from rainforests travels all around the world.

network, in which trees, especially in large rainforests like Amazonia, have always played a crucial part. Already our melting polar icecaps are a matter of huge concern … and the more we destroy trees, the greater the problem. Forests and jungles are crucial in the fight against global warming: they act as the 'lungs of the world', the breathing mechanism that maintains our sweet air, since trees provide the world with oxygen, while they absorb and store carbon from the atmosphere, helping to slow the rate of global warming.

Destruction of trees not only removes these 'carbon sinks', but if forests are cleared or burnt down, or even unduly disturbed so that they decompose, the trees' carbon intake is re-released as carbon dioxide, so that they pump even more of this greenhouse gas into the atmosphere. They also release methane, another gas whose excess is contributing to global warming. Conservationists are now warning that the healthy future of our planet is indeed in jeopardy.

Species Loss

This alarming rate of deforestation threatens many other wildlife species as, in turn, their habitat vanishes. There has been a sudden escalation over the last thirty years, with the extinction rate of plant and animal species taking place some 1,000 times faster than before humans emerged. Scientists fear that, over the next four decades, this may accelerate up to 10,000 times faster.

Vital resources are being plundered – as are countless animals, birds, insects and plants. Only extensive forest landscapes (or linked protected zones where animals can move through safely from one zone to

> Over a billion people depend on trees or the resources of forests for their livelihoods.
> In 1500 there were between 6 million and 9 million indigenous people inhabiting Brazilian rainforests; by 1900 there were only 1 million; today there are fewer than 250,000.

The effects of the destruction of a rainforest: over time other species disappear as their habitat is ruined, and the soil becomes dry, eroded and cracked.

another) can sustain healthy populations of larger animals like jaguars, bears, tigers and elephants – whose diminishing numbers alter the environment for all plants and animals in their locality. This also makes these threatened creatures ever more attractive to poachers.

Nonetheless, we continue to eliminate the habitats of creatures of all types, including useful insects as well as plants that may offer potential cures for life-threatening diseases. Despite the fact that 25 per cent of Western pharmaceuticals are derived from rainforest ingredients, as yet a mere 1 per cent of these tropical trees and plants have been tested for their medical attributes. For example, the US National Cancer Institute has identified 3,000 plants that are active against cancer cells; 70 per cent of these are found in the rainforest. So, as well as driving countless creatures closer to extinction, we weaken our own potential medical resources. In the process, we also wipe out indigenous peoples and their way of life.

Many believe that, unless there is some major reversal, the Earth is facing an extinction crisis. It is possible that our almost casual destruction of natural habitats will take millions of years to correct, and we shall probably never be able to rescue the vast species diversity that once flourished in relative obscurity within our forests. Intellectually, we should be aware of the shortsightedness of destroying trees at this rate; emotionally, we should be even more disturbed by this devastating loss. The grandeur, timelessness and sheer beauty of a tree, whether in a primary rainforest or blossoming at the end of our garden, should suffice to spur us on to take a stand in defence of trees, to uphold the forest and all its as yet undiscovered secrets.

Bibliography

Adams, Max. *The Wisdom of Trees: A Miscellany*. Head of Zeus.

Blackwell, Lewis. *The Life & Love of Trees: He who plants a tree, plants a hope*. PQ Blackwell.

Briggs, Gertrude. *A Brief History of Trees*. Max Press.

Davies, Gill and Gill Saunders. *The Romantic Language of Flowers*. Worth Press Ltd.

Deakin, Roger. *Wildwood: A Journey Through Trees*. Penguin.

Hight, Julian. *World Tree Story: History and Legend of the World's Ancient Trees*. Julian Hight.

Johnson, Owen. *Collins Tree Guide*. Collins.

Kirkby, Mandy and Vanessa Diffenbaugh. *The Language of Flowers: a Miscellany*. Macmillan.

Pakenham, Thomas. *Meetings With Remarkable Trees*. W&N.

— *Remarkable Trees of the World*. W&N.

Paterson, Jacqueline Memory. *Tree Wisdom: The Definitive Guidebook to the Myth, Folklore and Healing Power of Trees*. Thorsons.

Russell, Tony, Catherine Cutler and Martin Walters. *The Complete Encyclopedia of Trees of the World*. Lorenz Books.

Shanahan, Mike. *Ladders to Heaven*. Amazon Unbound.

Tudge, Colin. *The Secret Life of Trees: How They Live and Why They Matter*. Penguin.

Wohlleben, Peter. *The Hidden Life of Trees: What They Feel, How They Communicate – Discoveries from a Secret World*. Greystone Books.

Dench, Judi. *My Passion For Trees*. BBC Television documentary.

https://www.kew.org The Royal Botanic Gardens at Kew in southwest London house the largest and most diverse botanical and mycological collections in the world.

https://www.woodlandtrust.org.uk The Woodland Trust is the largest woodland conservation charity in the United Kingdom concerned with the creation, protection and restoration of native woodland heritage.

https://www.ted.com/talks/suzanne_simard_how_trees_talk_to_each_other 'How Trees Talk to Each Other', a Ted Talk by Suzanne Simard, Professor of Forest Ecology at the University of British Columbia, Vancouver, Canada.

Index

Picture Credits

123RF: Maksym Bondarchuk 39; Corey A Ford 60. **Alamy Stock Photo:** Maksym Bondarchuk 64, 67, 92, 115t; ClassicStock 134; dieKleinert 95; Florilegius 121t; Corey Ford 12; Helen Hotson 141; Sergey Mikhaylov 19; North Wind Picture Archives 147; Beryl Peters Collection 131b; WILDLIFE GmbH 126b; Zoonar GmbH 55. **Fotosearch:** arquiplay77 31, 108; cristi180884 59; Elenarts 88; LevKr 56; Nmorozova 23, 75, 83; VAC 51; zerbor 72;. **Getty Images:** Alan Baker 16, 114; Buyenlarge 137; DEA A. Dagli Orti 138; DEA G. Nimatallah 139; DeAgostini Picture Library 96, 97, 103, 132, 149; Historical Picture Archive Corbis 136. **iStock:** Allevinatis 81; annwaterru 127; AnYudina 122; arxichtu4ki 124t, 131t; bauhaus1000 2, 3, 17, 22, 28, 48, 52, 63, 73, 79, 80, 86, 91, 106, 107, 118t, 123, 129; cat_arch_angel 125; duncan1890 143, 144; Oksana Hlianko 128; ilbusca 77; Insdes 84; ivan-96 70, 89, 140; Mantonature 30, 90, 109; Max5799 130; NatuskaDPI 18; nicoolay 1, 10, 24, 29, 38, 41, 50, 66, 69, 74, 76, 78, 112; olgaserova 124b; Pobytov 11, 135; Ruskpp 126t; Tata_Pikulina 61; Thepalmer 112t; Tiana55 21; stdemi 94; WesAbrams 71; ZU_09 101; zzorik 120. **Missouri Botanical Garden:** 13, 20, 25, 45, 54, 62. **New York Botanical Garden:** 121b. **Shutterstock:** 3DMI 15; DK Arts 27. **Visipix:** 133. **Wellcome Collection:** 36, 98. **Worth Press Ltd:** 26, 32, 47, 68, 87, 99, 104, 110, 111, 113.